Broad Oak
A Kentish Village Reconsidered

By

Heather Stennett and K.H.McIntosh

The written word lasts

anon

ISBN No. 978-0-9544789-3-3

Published by K.H.McIntosh
for
The Society of Sturry Villages
Broad Oak House, 47 Sweechgate
Broad Oak, Canterbury
CT2 0QY
2006

THIRTEENTH CENTURY PEOPLE WITH BROAD OAK PLACE-NAMES
IN RENTALS IN THE BLACK BOOK OF ST. AUGUSTINE

Note: the final 'i' in writing numbers in Roman figures was usually rendered with a 'j' to emphasise it.

DE STURIA *(From Sturry)*
Redditus in festo sancti Michaelis (Rents at the feast of St. Michael -- 29 September)

Symon de Broko *(Maiton* added in a later hand)	xij *d*	12 pence
Iohanne de Kenebertelande	xxv *d*	25 pence
Amfridus de Kenebertelande	xij *d*	12 pence
Philippus de Kenebertelonde	vj *d* q°	6¼ pence
Robertus de Kenebertelond	vj *d* q°	6¼ pence

Rsdditus in festo sancti Andree *(Rents at the feast of St. Andrew – 30 November)*

Heredes *(The heirs of)* Yvonis de Kaldekote	xvj *d*	16 pence
Iohannis de Meytone	viij *d*	8 pence
Stephanus de Broderhok	vj *d ob*	6½ pence
Ricardus de Broderhok	ij *d ob*	2½ pence
Elyas de Meytone	vij *d ob*	7½ pence
Cristina de Swech	viij *d ob*	8½ pence
Willelmus de Swech	xj *d ob*	11½ pence
Iohanne de Kenebertelond	xij *d*	12 pence
Cecilia de Meytone	viij *d*	8 pence
Ysaak de Blakeslonde	xxvij *d ob* q° 27¾ pence	27 ¾
Askeetinue de Meytone	iiij *d ob* q° 4¾ pence	
Micahel de Kaldekote	j *d* q° 1¼ penny	
Heredes Iohannis de Broderhok	x *d*	10 pence
Gilebertus de Broderhok	ij *d* q°	3¼ pence
Elmerus de Broderhok	iij *d* q°	3¼ pence
Radulfus de Kenebertelond	xij *d*	12 pence

Redditus in aduincula beati Petri *(Rents at St. Peter in chains – 1 August)*

Iohanna de Kenebertelond	xxv *d*	25 pence
Amphredus de Kenebertelond	xxv *d*	25 pence

De redditu vomerum apud Stureye *(Concerning ploughshare-rents at Sturry)*

Heredes Roberti de Brodhoc et Goldwrod de Heye ad Pentecosten	iij vomeres

De clostura circa curiam de Sturea *(Concerning fencing around Sturry Court)*

Iohannes de Meytone et pares	ij virgatas et dimidium	= 2½ virgates
Iuhannes de Bradelonde et pares	j virgatam et iij quarteria	= 1¾ virgates, etc.
Amfredus de Bradelonde	j virgatam et iij quarteria	
Willelmus de Bradelonde et pares	iij quarteris et dimidium	
Iohannes de Kenebertelond et pares	virgatam , dimidium	
Yvo de Suech	virgatam et dimidiam, dimidium quarterium	
Bate de Suech	iij quarteria et pedem	
Heredes de Kaldekote	dimidiam virgatam	

These tenants of the Abbey had to share the cost of maintaining the wall or fence round the Court, apparently in proportion to the extent of their respective lands.

The definition of the <u>virgate</u> as a measure of length varies among authorities, from a yard of three feet to a rod, pole or perch of 16½ feet. The reference to Bate de Suech's three quarters and a foot suggests that the longer unit was intended.

The Place-Names of Kent

by J.R.Wallenburg
(Uppsala, 1932)

Belce Wood (6″): *de Bilichwode* (s. S.) 13th c. BlackBk; *de Bileche-*, *de Besechewode* 1249 ib.; *de Bylychewode* (s. Blengate hd) 1292 Ass. — A hill-name OE **Bylce* (late OE **Bylice*) + *wudu* "wood"? This name is perhaps connected with Bilchester in Hawkinge, v. *supra*.

Blaxland Fm 117 D 2: *de Blakeslaunde* 1226 Ass; *de Blaké(s)-londe* 13th c. BlackBk; *Blakeslond'* 1292 Ass; *Blakyslonde* 1308 AD, v. 6; *atte Blakelonde*, *de Blakyslond*, Joh. *Blake* 1332 Subs (s. Bleng. hd); *de Blakeslond'*, Th., Godeleua *Blak'* 1334 Subs (s. Bleng. hd); *de Blakislonde* 1346 Subs; *de Blakeslonde* 1347 Subs, etc. — OE *blæc* "black, dark", used as a pers. n. + *land*. There are indications that this name is of comparatively late ME origin.

Breadland Fms 117 D 3: *de Bradeland* 1226 Ass; *de Brodelond'*, *de Bradelande* 1240 Ass; *de Bradeland'*, *de Bladelande* 1254 Ass; *de Brode-*, *Bradelond(e)* 13th c. BlackBk; *de Bradelond* 1275 RH; *de Bradelond'*, *de Bardelonde* 1278 Ass; *de Bradelonde* 1313-4 Seld 24, 203; *de Brodelonde* 1327 Subs, etc. — OE *brād* "broad" + *land*.

Broadoak 117 E 2: *de Broderhok (passim)*, *del Brodhoc* 13th c. BlackBk; *Brodeoke* 1473, 1479 ArchC ex. v. II, 328-9. — OE *brād* "broad" (+ *ōra* "bank, border") + *hōc* "hook".

Buckwell 117 D 3: *de Bucwell'* 13th c. BlackBk; *de Buchewell'* 1254 Ass; *de Bokwell* 1306 Pat; *Bucwelle*, *de Bucwell'* 1313 Ass; *de Bocwelle* 1327 Subs; *de B(o)ukwelle* 1332 Subs; *de B(o)ucwelle* 1334 Subs; *de Bucwelle* 1338 Subs; *de Bucwell'* 1348, 1357 Subs, etc. — OE *bucca* "buck, male deer" + *w(i)elle* "spring, well".

Calcott 117 D 2: *de Kaldecote* 13th c. BlackBk; *de Caldecotes* 1278 Ass; *Caldecote* 1314 Pat; *de Caldecote* 1327, 1332, 1334, 1348, 1357 Subs, etc. — OE *c(e)ald* "cold" + *cot* "cottage".

Esseborne (lost): *Esseburnefeld* 1248 BlackBk; *Esseburnewode* 1249 ib.; *Es(se)burnefeld* 1251 ib.; *Asschbourne* 13th c. (?) ib.; *de Esseborne*, *de Esceburne* 13th c. ib.; *de Esseburn'* 1270 Ass; *Esseborne* Hasted, III, 613, x. — OE *æsc* "ash-tree" + *burna* "stream". This is probably the early name of the stream flowing through Sturry.

Hawe Fm 117 E 2: *de Haghe* 13th c. BlackBk; 1332, 1338 Subs; *(de) Hagh'* 1327 Subs, etc. — OE *haga* "enclosure".

Heel Lane (6″). Cf. perhaps *ate Helde* (s. Hawe) 1327 Subs. — OE *h(i)elde* "slope".

Hoades Court 117 D 3: *Hoad-Court* 1690 Ind Vill. — OE **hāþ* "heath".

Kemberland Wood (6″): *de Kenebertelande, -lond(e)* 13th c. Black Bk; *de Kenberste(s)lond* 1334 Subs; *de Kenebertelonde* 1338, 1348 Subs; *de Keneb'telond(e)* 1346, 1347 Subs, etc. — OE *Cynebeorht*, pers. n. + *land*.

Knowle Fm 117 D 2: *de Cnolle* 1254 Ass; *Knolle* 1408 Pat; *Knoll* 1502 Ipm. — OE *cnoll* "knoll".

Lynne Wood (6″). Cf. perhaps *Lenacre* (in S.) BM II (no reference). — The old form is OE *linæcer* "flax-field".

Mayton Fm 117 D 2: *(de) Meytone*, *Mayton'* 13th c. BlackBk; *de Meyton'* 1292 Ass; 1347 Subs; *de Mayton* 1308 AD, v. 6; *Meyton'* 1313 Ass; *de May-*, *de Meytone* 1332 Subs; *de Meyton* 1334 Subs; *Mayton* 1343, 1344 Cl. — The second el. is OE *tūn* "farm". The first el. is perhaps OE *mægða* "mayweed". Cf. Maytham in Rolvenden, v. *supra*. But OE *mæg* "male kinsman; female relation, woman, maiden" or *mægð* "maiden" may perhaps also be considered.

Sweech Fm (6″): *de Swech*, *de (la) Suech* 13th c. BlackBk (s. S.) — Cf. Sweech Fm in Elmstone, v. *infra*.

Thixlinge (lost). Compare *Tyxlynge* 1277 BlackBk; *de Thixling(h)e*, *de Tixling(e)* 13th c. BlackBk (s. S.); *de Tyxlinge* 1278 Ass (juror s. Bleng. hd). — The name is perhaps a toponymic, the base probably being the same as in OE *ðisl(e)*, *ðixl* "pole, shaft", the Ind Germ root of which (**tengh-*) is assumed to have meant "to draw, stretch, expand" (v. WP 1, 727). But the base may also be a nickname derived from the same base.

Calcott Hall, whose name derives from the thirteenth century's Michael de Kaldekote

A footnote to Wallenberg

By
Nita Bailey

The name Calcott probably comes from the Old English "Calde Cot" or "Cold Hut"; perhaps a shelter for animals in an exposed place. It could be that it has the same meaning as the more common "cold harbour" or "a place of shelter for wayfarers".

Mayton, the old manor house of which has been demolishd since the last war, comes from the Old English word "Maegoa", meaning "Mayweed". Not very far away is another even older manor site, that of Blaxland. This name, too, comes from the Old English "bloec", meaning" black, dark", used a personal name with the word "land" added. [The origin of the field name at Mayton of "How Hans" has been the subject of some speculation and may relate to there being a bank there.]

At the east of the main road going to Herne Bay and known as Foxhill (presumably because foxes lived there!) is Kemberland Wood. Cynebeorht is the Old English origin of this – another name with "land" added to it. It is easy to see how it became corrupted to Kembertisland and thence to Kemberland Wood. [There was an Abbot Kynebert at St Augustine's Abbey 874-879AD which may be the connection.]

Shelford used to be known as Shuldeford, and Barnet's Lane (the turning off Sweechgate) is a reminder that at one time much of upland Sturry was part of the vast Forest of Blean. The word Barnet comes from the Old English "Boernet", meaning "a burning or a clearing". Another small way in Broad Oak, unknown to most people, also has an Old English derivation. It is Heel Lane that branches off Mayton Lane, which in turn branches off Sweechgate at "The Golden Lion". The word "Heel" comes from "Hielde", meaning a slope and if you walk that way you will see that indeed Heel Lane does run across a slope of land.

Hawe Farm, the site of another old building and demolished more recently, was probably the successor of an even older building. Its name is also Old English in origin as Hawe derives from "Haga" which means "enclosure". The name of Lynne Wood at the top of Shalloak Road originates in the Old English "linoecer" or "flaxfield", a reminder that flax has been grown in these parts for a very long time.

Edited extract of an article in the Sturry Parish Magazine for March, 1966.

Photograph by courtesy of Allan Butler

The Footpaths of the Broad Oak Valley

By Monica Headley

While this article deals with the main routes crossing the Broad Oak Valley in all directions, further links can be made to show some connections with the old Roman road to Reculver. It seems certain that some of these tracks date back to the Stone Age, for archaeology has proved the occupation of this area continuously from that time.

Written histories relate the occupation by the Anglo-Saxons who bestowed their names on many of our villages and created so many of our boundary banks. This labour-intensive method was satisfactory for them and the banks have stood the test of time.

Sturry Footpath Group has been walking in the valley for over thirty years, and some of us were using these paths over sixty years ago. Naturally we know very thoroughly the intricate web of the Rights of Way which crisscross the area but there are still interesting discoveries to be made regarding their history and purpose.

There was part of one Right of Way that remained an enigma for a long time, and the puzzle was solved only very recently. The path, marked CB84 on the map, runs from behind Blaxland Farm south-westwards, through Cole Wood and curves round to emerge from the wood just below Brambles Farm. There it crosses the track and continues a short distance before stopping abruptly.

It is a safe assumption that a path has a destination as well as a good reason for following the route that it takes. We investigated this point, thinking that perhaps there had been some public building there, such as a mill, but there was no evidence to be found either on the site or in written records of there having been anything other than farm buildings.

We studied the large definitive map closely, (too closely, perhaps). Then the breakthrough came when we turned to the Ordnance Survey map and, at once, the larger picture sprang to life. On that map it was easy to follow the line westwards and see that an extension of this path would soon have reached the Radfall,(1) crossed it and continued from that point along the boundary between Chestfield and Hackington. Eventually it reverts to the status of Right of Way and emerges at the junction of Thornden Hill Road and Radfall Road. At this point it would be proper to say that it leaves the Broad Oak valley but it is our concern and interest to discover its final destination.

On the West side of that road junction a Right of Way continues. It crosses the disused railway and also the Old Salt Road and comes out on the Canterbury/Whitstable road just south of the Red Lion P.H. But that is not the end either. Almost opposite (and probably formerly directly opposite) a Right of Way continues, running south-westerly, crossing Denstroude Lane and after cutting off a corner, rejoins it again further on. By now the ultimate destination is clear. The most likely line is the south west course through north Bishopston Woods and Bossingden Wood taking a straight line (barring a recent diversion) to join the Roman road from

Canterbury to London (A2). An unexpected link with Broad Oak emerges: This final point is close to the source of the Sarre Penn,(2) the main stream that runs through the Broad Oak Valley.

The story of this Right of Way may be taken as an introduction to the fascinating subject of old routes and gives a fair example of how much it is possible to achieve by studying maps at home.

As a general principle, valleys usually have paths that follow the stream but, historically, the routes would lie above the floodplains, often one on each side of the valley. Of the other transverse paths here, the next south from CB84, is the route that begins along Mayton Lane, goes past Mayton Farm and Langton Lodge, (CB36) and comes out on Hackington Road. A branch turning left just after Langton Lodge then crosses the Radfall and eventually emerges on Tyler Hill. (Where it continues from there you may find out for yourself by consulting the Ordnance Survey map.)

Next south, and linked with the previous path in several places, comes Heel Lane (CB41). It leads down diagonally from a junction of three paths near the parish boundary, and is the only Right of Way to run along the bank of the stream (the Sarre Penn) as far as Tyler Hill.

If, (instead of cutting down to the stream) the path straight ahead is followed, keeping to the higher ground, it will be found to lead to Alcroft Grange and, changing its number to CB 44, to continue straight on to come out opposite Giles Lane and the University. The next path south is CB 46 from beside Mellow End in Shalloak Road, which joins the path from Heel lane and continues as CB 44.

The last transverse path from the high ground of Shalloak Road runs from beside Goose Farm (CB48). It had been a Bridleway (possibly even a Byway) but was downgraded to a footpath in relatively recent times. This path led directly across to Shelford Farm. Now it has been diverted on the west side of Beecham Wood, and skirts the quarry on an entirely new route. It still links with other Rights of Way, and it is possible to rejoin the original line at Brick House Wood, where it is still numbered CB 48. Beyond a confluence of routes, this path becomes CB 37 and continues close to the edge of the Hales Place estate in Hackington, joining the road a short distance up St Stephen's Hill.

The longitudinal (North/South) paths across the Broad Oak valley were links between the Stour valley and the North Kent coast, mostly via Herne. These vital routes were in use before the creation of the main Broad Oak to Herne Bay road. This road was turnpiked in 1813 but parts of it are much newer than the old ways which lie both West and East of it.

Beginning on the West side of the valley there is a path that branches from the route from Mayton Lane (CB35) and becomes CH1 as it crosses the Radfall boundary. From that point it makes a bold sweeping line north-eastwards to join

CH4 and continues in the direction of Herne via Bleangate and Braggs Lane. [Walkers beware! This not quite as straightforward as it appears on the map but an unmarked woodland track makes the walk possible.]

There are also other paths which join the main track towards Bleangate. Two of these pass Blaxland. One is a continuation of the road leading off Mayton Lane (CB84) and the other (CB88) divides from it and turns right near a stream. This appears once to have been a significant track, judging by its width and the avenue effect, with trees and a sparse hedgerow on either side of it. This route rises through an area which is often very water-logged. This may be the reason for the main approach to Blaxland having been changed to use the drier but steeper track which is now in use. The path, which was probably the original route (CB88) now swings right and passes in front of the site of Blaxland Cottage, now demolished.[4] Both these paths continue for a short length beyond Blaxland to meet another long distance path (CH2).

This path (CH2) links Warren Farm on Thornden Wood Road with Blaxland Farm. It then continues in a south easterly direction to meet the main road (A291). At that point the natural continuation is across the road to Woodlands Farm with the new number of CB54A, which links with the line of an old road which will be described presently. However, where the Right of Way (CH2) reaches the A291 it turns northward keeping inside the woods until it emerges almost opposite the Hicks Forstal Road.

Beside The Golden Lion Public House in Mayton Lane is a long path (CB71). It follows an almost straight line northwards to pass between Blaxland Farm and the site of Blaxland Cottages, retaining the same number (CB71) until it crosses the former parish boundary where it becomes CH4.

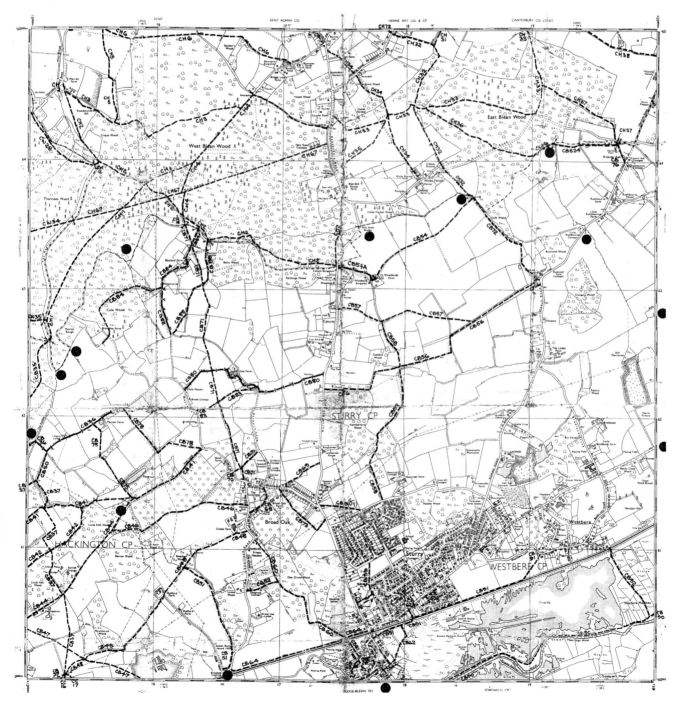

Near to The Golden Lion the route of CB71 is crossed by two short paths CB70 and CB83, both linking Mayton Lane with Barnet's Lane. Down in the valley there is a longer link from Mayton Lane via Vale Farm and on to the A291 main road. This link is a Bridleway. On the oblique opposite side of the road at the foot of Fox Hill, a Right of Way continues with the number CB56. However, the further continuation of CB56 is on a direct line with the Bridleway from Vale Farm, so it seems likely that in the past it continued straight across the line of the road.

The final story is about an old road which crossed the valley before the line of the present main road (A291) was established in that area.

The position of Woodlands Farm is adjacent to this old road. From the point where CB54A and CB54 cross at the old parish boundary point, the road seems to have continued its line, heading for Holy Sooly Bridge to meet the junction with Hicks Forstal Road. The position of Holy Sooly Bridge is marked on the Definitive Map but does not seem to be included in the Ordnance Survey. However, its position is still indicated by the way the main road – the A291 – sweeps in a very wide curve and passes to the west of the course of the old road. South of Woodlands Farm there was a house called Copt Hall, once the home of the Franklyn family and later the property of the church(3), demolished in 1963.

The line of the old road can still be seen even lower down the hill towards the Sarre Penn stream. Where it continued from there is difficult to say, although there are some indications which might eventually provide proof. The Right of Way which now continues the line is CB58. The road might have followed the same route, especially as the present footpath keeps to the line of an old (possibly Anglo-Saxon) boundary bank through Kemberland Wood on the Hawcroft Farm side of the valley. However, there has been within living memory a farm track leading up the hill from the valley bottom, right into the centre of Hawcroft Farm, and at the same time a wide path continued on the opposite side of the road (Hawe Lane). It was not then a Right of Way, but it was possible to walk through the wood to the point where the track met the Island Road, at Sturry (A28). This is put forward only as a possibility: perhaps further enquiry would reveal more evidence.

Everywhere we have found traces of the succession of people who have lived and worked here over the centuries and we feel awed to realise that we are walking where, as Gerald Manley Hopkins wrote, "generations of men have trod, have trod, have trod".

1. see "The Road Through the Woods" by Rudyard Kipling

2. "The Sarre Penn" by Jean Anthony, Allan Butler, M. Headley and Veronica Litten (1995)

3. "Sturry – the Changing Scene" ed K.H.McIntosh (1972)

4. "The Lost Cottages of the Broad Oak Valley" by

    Paul and Mary Crampton in this volume.

See also - Holmes, Wm. and Wheaten, Alexander (eds) THE BLEAN – The Woodlands of a Cathedral City. The Blean Research Group, Canterbury. (The White Horse Press, Ltd., 2002)

Broad Oak in Context

Broad Oak is part of the parish of Sturry, a large village to the north of Canterbury in East Kent. Too extensive to be considered a hamlet, Broad Oak is one of the original six boroughs of Sturry recorded in the Domesday Book in 1086 and identified as such by the Kentish historian Edward Hasted in his HISTORY OF THE TOPOGRAPHICAL SURVEY OF THE COUNTY OF KENT in 1778. As will be seen, the names of the landowners in the thirteenth century can still be identified without difficulty in the place-names of today – Gilbertus de Broderhok, Willelmus de Swech, Robertus de Kenebertelonde, Heredes de Kaldekote, Amfredus de Bradelonde and Johannis de Meytone – otherwise Broad Oak, Sweechgate, Kemberland, Calcott, Blaxland and Mayton.

Sturry itself is roughly the shape of a parallelogram bounded to the north by the ancient Forest of Blean and to the south by the river Stour. It is divided through the middle by the managed stream known as the Sarre Penn. The six boroughs (or markets) of which it is comprised are Broad Oak, (once known as Hothfield), Calcott, Blaxland, Sturry Street, (Street is the Anglo-Saxon name for a Roman road), Buckwell and Butland (which was until recently only commemorated in the name of the Westbere Butts Public House). This volume relates to the first three of these boroughs and should be thought of as in succession to the book STURRY – THE CHANGING SCENE (1972) which contains articles on Broad Oak and VILLAGE VIEWS (1988) which has many old photographs of the area. Other publications which concern the village are LETTERS TO STURRY by Monica Headley (2003), THE SARRE PENN by Jean Anthony, Allan Butler, Monica Headley and Veronica Litten, (1995) and IN GOOD FAITH – Twenty-Five Years of an Ecumenical Experiment (1995).

What is a Radfall?

By Harold Gough

Radfall - this strange word appears on the large scale Ordnance Survey maps of the area - Radfall, The Radfall, Radfall Road - but for most people nowadays, it is not the sort of word that crops up in everyday conversation. That is the result of the changeover that has taken place in the last two hundred years in the way of life of most people; from country dwellers to urban residents, and a simultaneous loss of woodland.

A farmer or village inhabitant in the past would have used the word as part of ordinary life - a term for a track though woodland, often between clearly artificial banks of earth lined with trees. Very often the track formed a parish boundary, well known from the annual 'Rambellation' - that Rogationtide perambulation of the borders of the parish, from one remembered mark to the next, recollected from youthful memories of being 'beaten' at each point.

The track was kept passable, for by what seems to have been a long-standing right, the locals were allowed to collect their winter fuel by cutting and gathering wood growing along it.

As for the true meaning or derivation of the word, dialect dictionaries are very little help. W. D. Parish and W. F. Shaw's Dictionary of the Kentish Dialect (1889) puts under "RODFALL — sometimes in a wood there is a belt of wood about a rod (161 feet) deep not belonging to the same owner as the bulk of the wood, and felled at a different time: as 'The wood belongs to Mus' Dean out there's a rodfall joins in with Homestall". Alan Major in his 1981 updated version simply repeated Parish and Shaw, without the quotation — not very helpful, either of them!

Hidden away in the big Oxford Dictionary, under "Rod", in the fifth column of closely printed usages, and headed 'special combinations' we find "rod-fall: **1664;** Agreement at Maldon, Essex, :land called Withers with ye rodfall and other appurtenances" and then Parish and Shaw again. Still no help.

The first thing to say is that direct observation shows that the width of these 'linear features' does not slavishly conform to the "rod, pole or perch" of $16^1/2$ feet some of us remember from schooldays — for a generation that missed 'Imperial' measures that is very slightly more than 5 metres. The track with or without banks, is not necessarily of that width, so neither the meaningless 'rad' nor the suggestive 'rod' seem relevant.

But there is another spelling that looks more hopeful. It is not just the boundary between Sturry and its neighbour to the west that has a Radfall, but a perambulation of the west part of Herne in 1791 mentions the word nine times in a short stretch of the boundary. Almost fifty years later, the Berne Tithe map and award of 1840 shows a narrow strip of land in that area called 'Road fall' but described as a 'shaw' or shelter-belt of trees separating the parish from the West Blean Wood. It is wide enough to be a track or road. So here we have a clue - rad or rod, now suggest a road perhaps. And fall, or fell, is to cut down timber. Many years ago I was told by a family of woodmen "When there is a roadway into the woodland that had to be kept open, the strip of woodland on either side was reserved for the upkeep of the roadway anything left was for the use of the people of the parish - they were apparently boundaries" A younger member of the family added: "They were allowed to cut the wood during the late autumn and winter, when the trees were not growing, and the field work on the farms was finished".

In the case of the local map, we find that much of Herne's boundary consisted of lengths of radfall. The section mentioned above divided Berne (territory of the Archbishop) from West BIean Wood (part of Chislet and thus property of St. Augustine's Abbey). It then continued in that way until it reached the eastern and northern sides of Thornden Wood, described by Hasted in his Survey of Kent in 1800 as part of 'the king's antient forest of the Blean'. Following Thornden Wood, it crosses the road from Herne Bay and meets the boundary of Swalecliffe, which in pre-Conquest times was also a property of the Archbishop.

Thus it seems that in many cases Radfalls are very ancient property boundaries, separating the terriories of great landowners, King, Archbishop and Abbot. In 949 AD a description of the bounds of the Archbishop's manor of Reculver, of which Herne was a part, reaching the point where the Radfall on the sides of Thornden Wood is reached, refers to 'cinges gemaere' - the King's boundary.

That same boundary, dividing Thornden from West Blean, also continues southward and separates Sturry from St. Stephen's, otherwise Hackington. Here we find the border between Sturry (St. Augustine's Abbey) and Hackington (the Archbishop). It is notable that in the north of Sturry where it meets the West and East Blean Woods, no physical boundary is necessary, for both Sturyagao and Chisteley came under the Abbey's jurisdiction as a single estate from the year. 605,two names for one property.

The identification of some Radfalls as parish or property boundaries, is confirmed in a recent paper by Tim Allen in *Archaeologia Cantiana*, cxxiv (2004) pps. 117-135, 'Swine, Salt and Seafood', in which he regards at least some radfalls as drovers' roads for moving pigs to the Blean woods for 'pannage', to feed on the fallen fruit of the woodland trees, as well as perhaps the transport of salt to Canterbury, based on recent archaeological work at Chestfield. He points out that as they define the boundaries of estates, parishes and woodland holdings, this is compelling evidence for their antiquity - which agrees with my own view of these tracks, and the evidence of that 10th century charter.

The Turnpike Road

By Sybil Kent

The Turnpike Road Plan from Sweechgate Cottage to Bleangate Cottage was published in 1813 and brought about the building of a new road down Fox Hill and up Calcott Hill past Holy Sooly Corner to Herne. The turnpike was in operation at Sweechgate and a toll was payable for anything on wheels going either to Herne Bay or down Sturry Hill to Canterbury. The usual charge was 1/2d (one halfpenny) per wheel, which would have involved the villagers of Broad Oak in considerable expense at that time had they not created their own footpaths to avoid payment of the toll. One of these, which is still in use, led from Broad Oak House down to Sturry; another went from Ilfracombe Cottage to the top of Fox Hill, both avoiding the toll-keeper. The only concession made by the authorities was to women with prams if they could stagger across the gateway with the pram in their arms.

The man responsible for the building and care of the gate was Edmund Keys, the wheelwright and claviger (or keeper of the keys) – an interesting occupational surname. His workshop and forge stood on the ground next to where the Broad Oak Hall stands today.

George Laslett, of Vale Farm (then called Hole Farm) and his wife Charlotte were once involved in a nearly fatal accident at the Turnpike. When driving home in a severe thunderstorm after visiting their Blaxland cousins at Whatmer Hall, Sturry, the horse bolted and leapt the Turnpike gate – a Turnpike gate is higher than a six bar gate - the top bar of which was broken by the force of the chaise wheel. The traces thus breaking released the horse which kept going. George and Charlotte were thrown out and were much injured. Their son Richard recorded in 1911 that he often looked at the repaired bar as he went past.

In November, 1877, the toll was abolished and the great gate which had stretched across the road was taken off its hinges and left to rot by the side of the road, a sight almost within living memory. Edmund Keys kept the foot-long cast-iron key until his death in 1927 and it was thrown away twenty years later by his daughter, Mrs Dorothy Baker of then number 13 Sweechgate Cottages.

The Way Through The Woods

They shut the road through the woods seventy years ago.
Weather and rain have undone it again,
And now you would never know
There was once a road through the woods
Before they planted the trees.
It is underneath the coppice and heath
And the thin anemones.
Only the keeper sees
That, where the ring-dove broods,
And the badgers roll at ease,
There was once a road through the woods.

Yet, if you enter the woods
Of a summer evening late,
When the night-air cools on the trout-ringed pools
Where the otter whistles his mate,
(They fear not men in the woods,
Because they are so few.)
You will hear the beat of a horse's feet,
And the swish of a skirt in the dew,
Steadily cantering through
The misty solitudes,
As though they perfectly knew
The old lost road through the woods. . .
But there is no road through the woods.

Rudyard Kipling

Published in *Rewards and Fairies* (1910)

Rudyard Kipling was a frequent visitor to Sturry Court where he stayed as a guest of Lord and Lady Milner after Lord Milner bought the estate in 1904/5. His daughter gave the editor of the Sturry Parish Magazine permission to publish the poem but could neither confirm nor deny that her father had had the old road through the woods from Broad Oak to Herne in mind when he wrote it.

Sweechgate Cottage at an unknown date

Photograph by courtesy of Gladys Robinson

Village Voices - 1

Edited extracts from an interview with Arthur Culver and his sister, the late Pearl Castle
by Heather Stennett on 27th April 2001

Where did you live when you were children?

Pearl Down Mayton Lane. Dad – he was Albert Henry Culver – was born in that house. It was a two up and two down and there was an old scullery out the back. Well, it brings it home to us what it used to be when we was kids, like. I used to sleep underneath the eaves, then there was Annie, then there was Kath and there was Frances. We was all in the same bed, sort of thing but I had to be under the eaves because I was the smallest one.

Can you remember the attic room?

Pearl There wasn't ever no attic, like.

Arthur It was a thatched house, wasn't it?

Pearl Yes.

Arthur With a scullery built on the other angle, like a wash house.

Do you mind me asking what the toilet arrangements were because people these days wouldn't know?

Pearl You went outside.

It was an outside one?

Pearl Yes.

Right. And was it one that your father emptied himself or did somebody empty it for you?

Pearl No, they had to empty it themselves, up the garden.

Arthur And the piss, you put it in there with ashes and you'd put it back on your garden. And it made lovely little taters, that did.

And what was the main form of heating?

Pearl There was just the oval stove and the oven.

And just thinking about day to day food, what kind of things did your family eat?

Pearl Well, Mum used to cook dinner, sort of thing. If Dad was home at dinner time, he had his dinner. Of course we had it in the evenings.

What kind of main food did you have then?

Pearl Grains, potatoes and peas, that sort of thing.

And your father grew them?

Pearl Yes. All in the garden.

How many were you in your family?

Arthur There was five girls and three boys. There was four boys, rather. He was Stanley.

Pearl He died when I was small and I could just start talking then. And I can remember them picking me up then looking in this box. Of course it was his coffin and he'd got a bunch of flowers on his chest. And of course [I was] just a little kid looking in there, sort of thing. It didn't register with me.

So how old was he when he died?

Pearl I think it was about ten or twelve.

And do you know what he died of?

Pearl Well, it was like Mum had a boy that was crippled and her sister, she had two boys that was . . . no, that's right, two boys that was crippled and they. . I suppose it was a kind of polio or something only they didn't call it that then. But there was several kiddies about Broad Oak like it.   [Other evidence suggests that it might have been muscular dystrophy]

If you could give us a bit of an idea where you came in the family, Pearl?

Pearl I was the youngest girl and I'm the one that's doing the most now.

And Arthur, where did you come in the family?

Pearl He was the. . .

Arthur I was the last boy.

Pearl You weren't the last boy, because Mum had [another] one.

Arthur I don't know, that was five then, wasn't it?

Pearl Yes.

Arthur Oh, yes, Mum lost one.

Pearl When she died the baby died with her.

Oh, so she died in childbirth.

Pearl Yes.

Arthur There was ten of them.

So how old were you then? Do you mind telling me your age now

Pearl No, I'm eighty. Last January.

And how old were you when your mother died in childbirth?

Pearl You was three, Arthur, weren't you? And I'm six years older than Arthur.

So you would have been about nine years old, right?

Pearl Right.

Your parents wouldn't have worked every single day. Was there anything special you did as a day outing somewhere or something special?

Pearl The only outing we went on was a Sunday School outing, and then when Aunt May come to live with us. . .

Who was Aunt May?

Pearl That was Mum's sister.

Arthur Only put a spell on you!

Pearl Yes, she would. And we used to have to go down to the wood, didn't we, to get a bundle of wood.

Arthur To keep the copper going or work down in the farmhouse.

Pearl All the other kids would be [going], because she used to make us go up there when all they, when all the kids were getting on the buses to go on these outings. Because we weren't allowed to go.

Why not?

Pearl Because there was no-one to look after us. There was all the mothers there, there was no-one to look after us.

So you were rather badly done by, then, not allowed to go on. . .

Pearl Yes.

Oh, what a shame. Can you remember any outing you went on before that?

Pearl We went on one tour, we went to Ramsgate, didn't we?

Arthur Yes. That was a long time ago.

Pearl Because he fell into the sea, didn't he?

How did you get there then?

Pearl Well we used to go on the buses, you see, buses and that. But as a rule they went to Whitstable, didn't they? Of course, then the time when he fell in the sea, because [our sister] Kath came with us then, didn't she, so we had to sit on the beach for him to dry hisself out.

Arthur They wrung me out two or three times.

I'm sure. So the furthest as a child you had been from here really was Whitstable and Ramsgate?

Pearl Yes

Did you get to Canterbury very often?

Pearl No. If we did go we had to walk. They done their shopping there what they couldn't get in Sturry

What sort of games did you play?

Arthur Rounders. Hot rice.

Hot rice?

Arthur Yes, hot rice.

Can you explain that to me? It's a new one to me.

Arthur You had the ball and the man that had the bat, or the child that had the bat, you threw the ball so that it hit him, and if it hit him he was out, and he'd strike the ball away, you see, with the bat. A bat similar to a bat and trap, the bat, wasn't it?

Pearl Yes.

And was the person with the bat allowed to move, or were they sort of frozen?

Arthur No, they just danced about, so you had a. . you know.

Pearl And then they had to run, didn't they?

Arthur Yes.

Pearl Round, in the square, sort of thing.

Were they allowed to run anywhere or were they limited as to how far they could go

Pearl You had the posts, sort of thing.

Arthur You had the posts, like rounders.

So, as I understand it, you have got the person with the bat and you're trying to throw it, they were standing in one, but running around, but your idea was to hit them with a ball, and they could fend themselves off with the bat.

Arthur Yes.

Oh, I haven't heard of that one before. I've played games similar to that, but I haven't heard it called hot rice. Was that a name just you think you called it, or was it all the kids?

Arthur No, it was a proper name for it and that's what we used to call it. And all the kids. And they used to go skipping, didn't they?

Pearl Yes.

Arthur You know there was a rope in the lane, you had … and we used to play "Granny over the ditch", didn't we? Up at the top of the lane.

Yes, what was that then?

Arthur Well, where the ditch is now, along by Port's at Goose Farm. . . So when somebody jumped over there after you, you jumped back to the other side so they couldn't catch you. . . there was water in there. There's still water in there now. Actually, the end of that ditch, round the corner there, it's got some watercress in it now.

Arthur, what was your first job?

Arthur On Brook's farm, picking up wood from behind the pruners, and then I went and worked with Dad with the horses, because they couldn't get no man to work with them, because they was all afraid of them, afraid of the horses. Like lambs, they was. But they jigged about a bit, you know. Stood on their hind legs, and that. There was three horses. .

What kind of things did you have to do with the horses?

Arthur Ploughing, plough the fields and bulk them up, which is a bulker is what you stroke potato furrows with. We used to do it all between the bushes with that, then split them. The furrows we

done all right round the barn, we got them all up like to a point, right down to the bushes, and then when we got right round, the wheels was each side of that and then it spilled it open, the field that the furrows in and then you went with a shim with diggers on, which you had to carry the thing the whole time on your shoulders, and that used to break them down and then after that you had wide, broad plates on that ran through the ground and didn't go any further in the ground, and it would stop the horses, like a handicap, so we had to carry them all the time. It was jolly hard work, that was. The bulkers and the plough ones were hard work, because you grind them round at the end and turn them round

So when did they go over to mechanical tractors then? I mean, when did they stop having horses?

Arthur It was after the war.

What other work was there in the village before the war?

Arthur There was a carpenter's shop making wheels and stuff like that for carts.

A wheelwright's?

Arthur A forge.

Pearl And down Mayton Lane there was a lot of woodwork.

Arthur A woodyard.

Pearl And a market garden. You know, a nursery. A chicken farm – and picking blackcurrants.

Tell me about Aunt May. It sounds as if she was a bit of a tartar.

Pearl She was more than a tartar, wasn't she?

Arthur Yes. I'm afraid she wasn't a very nice lady.

Pearl And if she could get you into trouble she would.

Arthur And she'd hit you with a bloody stick. I'd be polishing that old kitchener in there, and she's been hitting me over the back with her stick. "Oh, you've missed a bit." like that, and then, when you'd finished she'd sit in the chair and light her pipe, and spit all over it, wouldn't she?

Pearl   Yes.

Was she active herself?

Pearl   No.

Arthur   She could have been.

Pearl   Well, she could have moved if she liked but she didn't like. Everyone waited on her.

Arthur   We used to have to carry her upstairs, you know. That was handy. So we used to carry her up feet first so her head was downhill. So if she don't keep quiet. . .

Have you any memories of war-time Broad Oak?

Arthur   When Albert [his brother] was home on leave and the Germans came over and we was down behind The Golden Lion, we put up a rabbit out on the plunge down there, and it run down there in the ditch to earth and we put the ferret down there and whilst we was doing that the Germans came and shot the hedge to pieces, what was landside. These was actually like pieces and we was laying beside that, laying along here, and that hedge was shelled to bits. Then when we got home the roof was all to pieces where a shell had hit the roof and all.

Pearl   It was Beryl, you know, Topsy's Beryl. She was out behind the door, and Ella Gammon grabbed her in. And if they'd turned, because they saw her, or else, and they were coming straight through our window. But they turned in time, shooting all the time, but of course they didn't get the chance, because Ella had got her.

Arthur   Yes, we was there. We all laid along this hedge and a bomb

dropped up by Little Orchard just across the road from that, and it bounced, and then it came just over the wire like that and exploded just in the orchard beside us. It was only for the fact that we was down below the bank because there was this ditch there, and there was a hedge, and there was a ditch the other side. It sloped over to the hedge and that's where we laid down, and of course it was above the bank about that much. And then this bomb went off and chucked everything all over us and then we came home after that, you know.

And there were some unexploded bombs dropped on the village as well, I believe

Arthur   Yes, I mean, one under your house, Heather, and the other one out where I think the third bungalow along, where old Stan used to live, because there was a pond out there. It dropped in there and then kept going. The weight of the bomb, you know, it kept going, it crept right down under your house. They could've hidden it, that one. They had a hell of a job getting that one out. Because they evacuated us because the bombs was there, because we lived close by and then brought us home to see them go off.

I know that Mrs Pout wasn't allowed to sleep in her house but she was allowed to go up the field to feed the pigs and be in the house all day, so why they thought the bomb would go off in the dark I just don't know.

Arthur   Yes, a bomb dropped that Saturday afternoon in Goodburn's garden, didn't it?

Pearl   Yes.

Arthur   And then all them bombs bounced because the aircraft was that low. They went right down just above

the hedges. And of course the bomb went down like that, it bounced and went up in the air again, and then down. And then there was another dropped in the orchard by Sturry Wood, in the plums, and that dropped down by Mellow End, and then bounced again and out into Port's field.

Was anyone injured by any of these attacks

Arthur   There was an East Kent bus shot-up, wasn't there, down Fox Hill. And there was another one along Sturry Road shot up to pieces as well

Yes, my grandmother was on that bus and she had to get out past people who were very badly injured and dead.

Tell me, did you get up to any mischief?

Arthur   There was this old chap that had a pen, a big coop and it was like this room, built in briar, then he had three tunnels that went in there like wire netting. His pheasants used to squeeze through then they couldn't get back. They went in like and shut up, like that. Me and Frank Macey was up round there. We used to go and see if there was any pheasants in there. Because there was a door there to get in there and we'd soon have them out. He used to have a big old dog, didn't he? An Old English sheepdog. When we saw that about we scarpered, you know.

Pearl   Got out of the way quick. And this old man, we'd been primrosing, Frank and I, and we came out of the wood and this old man was chasing these pigs round the stack, where there was double stacks, sort of thing. Of course they then dived

---

Acknowledgements

Jean Anthony
Diana Brown
Allan Butler
Derek Butler
Hazel Castle
David and Jan Clover
Trevor and Carol Davis
Iris Garwood
Jan Gaskell
Harold E. Gough

Winifred Harvey
David Howard
Colin and Mary Kennett
The Kentish Gazette
Ellen Luke
Ian B. Moat
Sarah A. Perry
Kenneth Reedie
Margaret Sangster
Kenneth Westwood

And especially Robin Edmonds for all his help with the photographs and Leslie Moran for the field-map.

We would like to thank everyone for the overwhelming support we have been given and the wealth of information shared with us. We are only sorry we cannot print it all. Human memory is, alas, not infallible and some reminiscences of an event may not be the same.

Broad Oak in the Nineteenth Century

By Anne Oakley

In 1871 Edward Seward at Vale farm employed eight men and two boys on 205 acres. His farm bailiff, William Hooker, also lived there with his wife Esther and two farm servants. James Fleet is described as a farmer and the owner of 209 acre Hawe farm. Robert Mount at Sweech farmed 115 acres and employed three men and a boy, but also had one farm servant, and a domestic servant to care for his twins Esther and Robert aged two. William Austen also farmed at Sweech where he lived with his wife Maria, his grandson Henry Grant and his granddaughter Sarah Miskin

There are only 28 agricultural labourers listed in this year as against the 58 accounted for in 1851, and five farm servants, as against the very large number in 1851, but there were others reliant on the farmers: four woodmen, ten casual labourers, including one woman! Esther Burton, a widow with four children under eleven and her mother to support; two blacksmiths, two waggoners and their mates, a wood-reeve and a gamekeeper. Others served the local community: a dressmaker, two needlewomen, six carpenters, a sawyer, two roadmen, a grocer, a publican, a pork butcher living at home with a farm labourer and his wife, one man working in the gravel pit, and a shoemaker. One woman, Mary Stuart, was living 'on the parish', and three others are described as infirm or invalids, unable to work

Fifty four of the 82 households had children living at home. Of these 159 children, 102 are described as scholars though it is doubtful that they all attended school all at the same time. Some left at 12 but others were still there at 16, presumably helping as monitors. Only 20 children had attended when the school opened in 1851. A few families were large: John Fox and his wife Sarah had nine children; and George Rowsell and his wife Sarah had eight. Otherwise there were two families with six, four with five, seven with four, sixteen with three, nine with two and the rest with one - an average of three to each family. In 1851 there had been 199 children belonging to 65 families in much the same ratio and of these 51 were then under three years of age.

In many cases in the 1871 census wives were older than their husbands, and this 1S true of 22 of the families living in Broad Oak. Sarah Fox was five years older than her husband and had her youngest child when she was 44. The family had settled in Broad Oak only two years before, and had otherwise moved from Fordwich to Canterbury St Paul, Whitfield, and Eythorne beforehand. Ann Castle was seven years older than her husband James and had her last child, Charlotte, at age 47. All her six children were born in Sturry, and there may have been others who had already left home. Some families had relatives living with them to provide for or support or give a home. Henry Alderton, the gamekeeper, had his mother-in-law, Ann Jones, a needlewoman aged 50 and his wife's sister Mary A Jones then 17, a dressmaker living in. Edward Seward had his eleven year old nephew Edward Elgar; and William Austen his grandson and granddaughter. James Barnett and Susannah had their granddaughter Sarah Millgate. Others had boarders, mostly farm labourers in-coming without families, and domestic servants. George Marsh, a widower aged 40, had returned to live with his parents Henry and Hannah. George worked as a waggoner for

his father who was a farm bailiff, and his younger brother William, then 15, was his mate. Another brother Henry, then 35, was visiting for a few days from Herne. Hannah Kellick's husband had gone to sea leaving her with two children at school. Ann Blackman had remarried and now kept a grocery business to support her older children and the two very young ones.

Many of the younger children were born in Sturry or Broad Oak, but their parents had often come from far away places out of Kent as well as the many Kent parishes. Henry Alderton had come from Farnham in Surrey, and his wife's family from Brampton Brien in Hereford. Tuth Pickup, a domestic servant at Sweech farm, came from London.

William Bednay, a brickmaker and his wife Elizabeth from Ryton near Coventry; John Piper, an agricultural labourer, from Playden in Sussex; and Benjamin Bond, and his wife Frances from Ipswich with a son born in Sheerness. William Hooker, farm bailiff at Mayton , came from Hoath with his wife; Edward Seward from Dover; Robert Mount from Eythorne; James Fleet from Canterbury and his wife Ann from Ramsgate; William Keys and Hannah Kellick from Broomfield; William Rye, a brickmaker's labourer, from Boughton, but his wife from Westminster; William Austen came from Wye but his wife from Berkshire. Others came from literally all over Kent. Few stayed permanently.

By 1891 there had been changes. The 82 households including Sweech, Hawe, Blaxland, Mayton, Vale, Mount Pleasant, Goose and Broad Oak farms were still working farms and absorbing much of the local working male population, but there was also a certain amount of diversification. Stephen Bean was living at Sweech as farm bailiff with his wife Emma and their son William, then 19, who was employed as a farm servant, his daughter Edith Emma, and two boarders, also farm servants. William J Austen and his elder brother George were running the farm and lived there with Mary Ann, William's wife, and their six children. James Fleet was still at Hawe farm with his growing family of two sons and four daughters aged between 19 and 27, and two young domestic servants. James now described himself as a brewer and farmer. Robert Tumber farmed Mayton with his wife, daughter in law, grandson and four live in boarders. James Bubb, a shepherd, was running sheep at Blaxland and lived there with his wife and eight children, two of whom were helping on the farm. James Tharp, the blacksmith was now also a farmer and also lived at Blaxland. Laura Hurley, a widow, farmed at Vale with her nine year old son Vivian, Henry Holness, her farm bailiff, and a domestic servant. Nearer to the centre of the hamlet Alfred Britcher and his wife Sarah ran Broad Oak farm; and Henry Hall ran Goose farm with three farm servants. Both Alfred and Henry were farm bailiffs.

The number of available agricultural labourers had by now risen from 28 in 1871 to 75. Men still relied on the availability of farm work, but it seems that a decline was beginning to manifest itself. A large family of woodmen had recently moved into the hamlet, all members of the Keen family, who lived near one another in a close knit group. They were joined by George Mutton and Charles Knight. There were also two timber merchants benefiting from their labours, and although there had been woodmen previously, their numbers had been smaller. Added to this grouping there were also five carpenters, a rough carpenter and his journeyman son carpenter, two apprentice carpenters and also a wood-turner. There was work for these men in repair work and building. Gardening was another outlet: as well as a market gardener there were four gardeners. The railway was also providing work for a platelayer and a clerk. In a few years time the gravel pits would provide work for many men, but at this time only one worked there. Laythorne (Latham) Blackman was running the grocery, bakery and butchery business started by his mother Ann around 1830 with his wife Sarah as the baker; and Adam Ingleton was farming Goodwin as well as running the Golden Lion public house.

In 1891 there were 65 families with children. Families ranged in size from one child to eight but the average of three children per family remained the same.

Of the 198 children living in Broad Oak 49 were under three years of age, and 49 others were attending school. Others were living at home as domestic servants or working elsewhere though some daughters seem to have had no occupation at all. Seventeen relatives from elsewhere were living with families, some very young, some working; two were supporting aged fathers.

During the 1870s and 1880s there were brick-makers and bricklayers working in Broad Oak, and perhaps some of them were employed in building the smaller houses, though the new Broad Oak House had been built by Henry Miskin in 1862, later occupied by Robert Dixon, his wife and son. Robert was a rich man of independent means who was born in the city of London in 1841. As a young man of 26 he was in South Australia, perhaps as a potential settler in Adelaide where only settlers were sent, never convicts. In about 1866 or so he married his wife Fanny from Norwood near Adelaide, and two years later they had a son John C Dixon who was born there. Eventually the family returned to England where John became a theological student, and perhaps yearning for open spaces such as are found in Adelaide, decided to settle in Broad Oak. They lived in the house from about 1888-1898. In 1899 it was bought by Captain A Gordon Inglis. This house was a very modern property for Broad Oak, large and almost entirely out of keeping with others in the hamlet. It was a portent of what was to happen in many Kent villages and hamlets in the years ahead.

Sources: Census for Sturry 1851, 1871, 1891; Directories and Blue Books.

Broad Oak Chapel Christmas Party circa 1950

Front Row: John Colley, Colin Reeves, Michael Gisby, Tony Whittaker, John Wellard, David Sparkes, Colin Thompson.

Second Row includes: Jean Giles, Sophie Beaney, Sandra Cowley, Mr and Mrs Lawrence Russell from Herne Bay Court, Janet Harwood, Linda Kennett, Pamela and Raymond Beecham

Third Row: Jasmine Ward, Jean Wellard, Norma Baker, William Harwood, Barry Ward, Joyce Wellard, Betty Kemp, Mary Colley, Sylvia Beaney, Angela Cowley

Back row: Sarah Webb, Heather Baker, Ivy Birch, Marion Jones, Barbara Beecham, Janet Moran, Iris Kennett, Jean Webb

Mellow End

Signed Drawing of a house in Broad Oak by T.S.Cooper dated 1833, possibly Mellow End. There is, alas, no mention of it in his 2 volume autobiography MY LIFE published by Richard Bentley and Sons, 1890

One of Broad Oak's saw-pits used to be in front of this old house at Mellow End. The other was beside what is now the site of the Broad Oak Hall, where Adam Ingleton, Mine Host of The Golden Lion, had his business as a wheelwright and carpenter and where Edmund Keys worked. The sight of the great cartwheels made by Edmund Keys being wheeled across to where Dorinda Cottages now stand was once a common one. There stood a forge owned by the Tharp family and later by a Mr Gillingham where hot iron bands were hammered onto the cartwheels. The saw-pit at Mellow End was owned by a Mr Carmichael and three generations of the Culver family were at some time sawyers here: William Culver (1781-1857), James (1816-1900) and Thomas, a timber merchant, (1846-1891). William was the grandfather of Henry James Culver, (1842-1932) whose obituary appears in this book and the great-great-grandfather of Albert Culver and Pearl Castle interviewed in "Village Voices One" also in this volume . The early photograph is thought to be of either William Culver and his wife, Jane, or his son James and his wife Mary. The house and outbuildings were also thought to be the subject of the sketch dated 1833 by the artist Thomas Sidney Cooper, who owned much property locally. It is reproduced here by kind permission of the Royal Museum at Canterbury.

Mellow End formerly known as Culver's Orchard.

Carrie, Jessie and Walter Culver photographed outside Milboroughs sometime in the nineteen twenties in a car thought to be a Morris Oxford with a two unknown passengers and driver.

DEATH OF MR. H. CULVER.

STURRY'S OLDEST INHABITANT.

We regret to record the death of Mr. Henry Culver at the advanced age of eighty-nine years. Mr. Culver, who was the oldest inhabitant of the parish of Sturry, died at his home at Broad Oak on Sunday night. He leaves a widow, four sons and four daughters, twenty-four grandchildren, and three great-grandchildren.

Mr. Culver was born in 1842 and lived in Broad Oak during the whole of his long life. He was a carpenter and wheelwright by trade, and, in his later years, worked for Lady Drummond in the Broad Oak Lodge gardens, when that house was being used as a convalescent home for wounded officers.

Had he lived until July he would have celebrated his diamond wedding, for it was on July 4th. 1872, that he married Miss Pout. Mrs. Culver was nurse and midwife in the parish for thirty-three years, and there are few people in the district who cannot look back and recall with gratitude one of her kind actions.

Mr. Culver was a fine old man, and, until recent months, was comparatively alert and active. He will be greatly missed by his many friends and relatives.

:o:

Death of Mr H Culver

Broad Oak Chapel

By Robert Collins

The chapel at Broad Oak came into existence due to a policy of "home mission" being carried out by the Countess of Huntingdon Congregational Church in Watling Street, Canterbury. Under the leadership of the Reverend Valentine Ward, church representatives were sent out from the city to preach in several of the nearby villages. The visits to Broad Oak were entrusted to Mr. William Acomb, a lay preacher of that church. He began his work in October 1866 and quickly discovered that, unlike other places on his itinerary, many people in the village desired a place of worship. Several village meetings were held to discuss this ambition and in January 1867 a local landowner, Mr. William Austen, offered a piece of ground on which to build a village chapel. Work began on July 10th, 1867 and the building must have been completed exceptionally quickly as the official opening took place just over a month later on August 14th, the formalities being carried out by the Reverend Valentine Ward with 160 people in attendance. The event was captured in a remarkable photograph taken just outside the chapel. One hundred and sixty persons was a large number of people for such a small building (Acomb wrote that it was "crowded to excess"), and over the following months it became clear that the chapel could not accommodate everyone who wanted to attend. Fortunately, Mr Austen allowed the further use of his land to extend the building a further 13 feet at the rear. A Sunday school was also started; a year later the summer school treat was attended by 80 children.

Although both the Reverend Mr Ward and William Acomb left the Canterbury area in 1870, the chapel continued to be overseen by the church at Watling Street. However, the day-to-day running of the place was carried out by a group of local people from Broad Oak and Sturry.

A generation after its opening the chapel was proving quite an expensive building to maintain - the roof had to be completely renewed in 1882, and chapel funds were often very tight. Much of the monies needed to keep the chapel in working order had to be raised by local subscription. At this time there were two services on a Sunday - one at 10:30am, then again at 6pm, taken by the minister from Watling Street. Unfortunately by the 1890s there were very few people associated with the managing of the chapel, although those few that were involved were very devoted to the work.

Among these were Mr. Laythorne Blackman of Sturry, who in 1895 became the chapel superintendent, and Mr. Albert Curd of Broad Oak who became the secretary. There were also regular visiting speakers to the chapel. Reverend William Edmondson became minister of the Watling Street church in 1896, and from the very start of his 21~year ministry took a keen interest in the work at Broad Oak.

The Sunday school treat became a regular event for the village; at first this was held locally but in later years would be held at both Herne Bay and Whitstable. The Sunday school held an annual prize-giving session from 1898 to reward the most regularly attending Sunday school scholars. After negotiations with the appropriate landowners, the chapel was

Broad Oak Chapel Prize Giving
Among those present were Mrs Martha Grier, Ron Barnard (always known as Uncle Ron), Mrs Migs Clark (wife of the Minister, the Revd Jonathan Clark), and their daughter Debbie, Janine Jenkinson, Robert and Elizabeth Collins, Timothy Clements, Colin and Carol Clarke, and Daniel and Vicky Wood.

Photograph by Kentish Gazette

further enlarged slightly at the rear in the spring of 1899. At the turn of the century, an attendance of around 100 people could be expected. The 1905 Sunday school treat was a very grand affair; judging by the photograph of the occasion, seemingly the whole of Broad Oak village coming to wave

Broad Oak Chapel in 2000, Allan Butler outside

Photograph by Don Bridges

Photograph by courtesy of Frances Moore

**Mr. Kirby at the pulpit
of the Strict Baptist Chapel in Sturry. C 1932**

The only known view of the interior of the Strict and Particular Baptist Church in Sturry High Street, destroyed by bombing in November 1941, photographed by her aunt Joan Parnell when on holiday in Herne Bay in 1932.

off the party on their way to Whitstable. Mr. Amos Baldock of Tyler Hill supplied his traction engine to transport the three large cartloads of people to the coast. By all accounts the trip was a very popular one and an identical visit took place the following year.

Photograph by Mrs Ellen Todd

Broad Oak Chapel Christmas Party in the Hall circa 1960

Among those present were Mrs Alexandra Hill, Mrs Ellen Todd, Mrs Martha Grier, Mrs Mabel Dunn, Mrs Jaqueline Wilkinson, Mrs Margaret Martin, Pat Gower, Janet and Alan Todd, Janice, Kevin and Roger Gower, Lesley, Christine and Vanessa Patey, Susan and Sally Reynolds, Lynda Grier, Diana Richardson, Martin and Melvyn Bacon, Liz and Brian Thompson, Carol Lawrence, Christine and Robert Keen, Louisa Smith, Christine Wilkinson, and Beth Wallace.

MR & MRS HANCOCK   MR & MRS KIRBY   MR. MOAT   MR. L. JARVIS

Photograph by courtesy of Frances Moore

Preacher and members of the congregation of the Strict and Particular Baptist Church at the back of the Chapel in 1932 – Marcus Hancock, (died 1938), Caroline Hancock (nee Dunn), F.J.Kirby, Mrs Kirby, Josiah Moat, Deacon of the Church who ran the Canterbury to Herne Bay horse-bus Tally Ho!, and L.Jarvis

When war broke out in 1914, services were suspended and the chapel was commandeered by the War Office, who paid £29 7s 6d for the use of the building as a military sickbay. (Many years later, some World War One uniform buttons were found in the chapel field opposite and are now on permanent display). Albert Curd left the chapel in 1916 and William Edmondson died the following year, leaving a new generation to see the chapel into the post-war period.

When the chapel reopened after the war, attendance at services and the Sunday school had declined considerably. Edmondson's successor was Reverend Alexander Snape, a headmaster-turned Congregational Minister who, like his predecessor, paid great attention to the work at Broad Oak. Under his guidance, the chapel was steered through quite a lean period following the Great War. He left the area in 1926.

When the Broad Oak Village Hall was built in 1928 there was a strong link between the two buildings; one of the driving forces behind the Village Hall, Mr. Ernest Stennett, became leader of the chapel Sunday school for the next seven years. It was another prosperous period for the school, which had 76 scholars on the books in 1933. The chapel installed gas lamps in 1935.

During the Second World War, the chapel's parent church at Watling Street was completely bombed during two air raids in June and October 1942. Nevertheless, the chapel again thrived during difficult times. In the absence of an overseeing Watling Street minister (who had resigned in 1940), Mr. Maurice Cooper and his wife were leading a very successful chapel Sunday school. However, as before, after the war there was a decline in adult support. This appears to have occurred quite swiftly as by the end of 1950 the chapel was almost abandoned and closed, and although this did not happen, Mr. Cooper described 1952 as "a difficult year in an apathetic village". Then came Mr. Laurence Russell and his wife from Herne Bay Christian Conference Centre, who enjoyed a very successful five-year stint in charge, drawing much praise from the new minister and congregation at Watling Street church (in a temporary building from 1948-1955 when work on the new church started.) Several Sunday school outings took place to the Christian Conference Centre, still in use today.

Mr. Russell officiated at the first marriage to take place at the chapel - on August 15th, 1959, between Doris Mayo and Stanley Thompson. The chapel appears to have become detached from its parent church at Watling Street by the end of the 1950s, which again left it without a minister. But over the next few years a very dedicated group of local helpers moved in to administer the Sunday school, including Mrs. Agnes Pout (the granddaughter of Mr. Austen), Mr. Ted Todd & Mrs. Ellen Todd, Mrs. Martha Grier, and Mrs A Hill. An outdoor toilet was installed in 1962, with running water supplied in 1966 when the area at the rear of the building was converted into a kitchen. A "restoration fund" was launched that year to try and deal with some structural failings (the chapel has always suffered from damp), with the chapel floor being heavily treated. Sixty scholars regularly attended the Sunday school in 1968.

Mr. Andrew Reed, a trainee minister, had filled the pulpit as often as he was able from 1963 to 1967, but thereafter the chapel was without a regular minister until September 1972 when Reverend Tom Cooper of Herne Bay arrived. This was the first time the chapel had had its own minister independent of Watling Street. He remained in charge until his death in June 1981, and then numbers started to decline. The chapel was again without a minister, and although the Sunday school continued (largely thanks to the wonderfully dedicated Mr. Ron Barnard of Tankerton who ran the school from 1980 until 1995), the adult attendance was very low (dropping to just two in 1985) which seemed to mean that the chapel would have to close. However, in recent years, Reverend Jonathan Clark (1987-1992) and Reverend Ted Hamer (Since 1992) have held dedicated ministries and the chapel is again playing a part in the life of Broad Oak village.

This was written by Mrs. Agnes Pout at an unknown date

The Oast and Ilfracombe House in Sweechgate before the building development in the nineteen-thirties.

Photograph by courtesy of Allan Butler

One Hundred Years Ago

Tug O'War team and spectators.

Photograph by Jan Gaskell

A series of excellent sports were held in connection with the parishes of Broad Oak and Sturry on Thursday. The competitions took place in Mr Maxted's meadow at the top of Sturry Hill, and were watched by a large crowd. The feature of the event was a tug-of-war. The Broad Oak team, under the command of Mr Terry, Superintendent of the Canterbury Sewage Farm, carrying all before them, beat the Canterbury Gas Works and also the 7th Dragoon Guards

Mr George Uden, of Calcott, had an unfortunate accident on the aerial railway. He collided heavily at the end of one of the journeys and broke a bone in one of his legs.

From The Kentish Gazette, October 6th, 1906

The Siege of Goose Farm

Towards the end of September, 1905, a market gardener called Arthur Minter saw this advertisement in the Kentish Express:

'To let, Goose Farm, Broad Oak, Sturry, about three miles from the city of Canterbury, consisting of capital farmhouse and ample buildings, together with 76 acres of arable and pasture land. Rent £100 per annum.'

The tenant of Goose Farm when Arthur Minter saw the advertisement was called Clark. And the first thing Minter did after seeing the agents was to call on him - when he found the buildings in a sad state of disrepair. Clark had been there as a tenant for eight years and warned Minter to get everything done up when he came in because he would get nothing done by the agents after. Minter asked Thomas Wacher, J.P., the agent, for a seven-year lease but was told he could only have the farm under a three-year agreement. Minter said he would take it "on custom of the country" terms - that is the agent to put the place into good tenantable condition, and find material, and the tenant to find labour afterwards to keep it up. He took possession in the first week of November, 1905, moving his farming tackle in with his own men and horses, and the assistance of a traction engine and three trucks. Clark, the outgoing tenant, is said to have prophesied "Minter may want a traction engine to move him in but I bet he will not want a traction engine to move him out".

The Tenants' Rights Valuation (that is what was owing to the outgoing tenant for agreed improvements) was carried out by two men called Finn and Charles Petley. They assessed Clark's Tenants' Rights at £140 . Wacher, the agent, allowed Minter £40 for thatching the barn and doing up the fence between Cow Lees and Hatch's field (just over the brow of the hill) but told him on no account to pay any of the £100 over to Clark, to whom it rightfully belonged as he hadn't paid his rent and it was to go towards this.

By this time Arthur Minter had done a bit of asking around and found that the landlord of the Shelford estate of which Goose Farm was then a part was a man of straw called Aylwin who was being pursued by his creditors. Minter therefore declined to pay over the balance of £100 on the grounds that if he himself gave up the farm and they couldn't get another tenant, he wouldn't be able to recover his valuation. This did not go down well with Wacher, but he agreed to let it stand over, with Minter paying 5 per cent interest on the money.

At the end of September that year, Wacher sent Minter a notice giving him twelve months' Notice to Quit, with a covering letter saying that if he paid the £100 by the following August, he would be very pleased to withdraw the notice. Minter paid his annual rent due at Michaelmas and nothing happened until January, 1907, when Wacher summoned him to his office and tried without success to get Minter to sign a promissory note for the £100.

A notice of half-year's rent was sent that April but Minter did not pay it. A few days later he looked out of the window of Goose Farm and saw three men approaching the front door. They were sent round to the back door when one of them said "I am Edwin L.Gardner, a County Court Bailiff, and have come here to distrain for £50 due to Mr Thos Wacher as agent for the landlord, Mr F.W.Aylwin. Minter demanded to see his certificate for doing this. He hadn't got it and had to send his man, Ratcliff, back to Canterbury for it. The others all had a jug of ale. When he came back, Minter asked Gardner to get on with his business and distrain in the proper way. When he had done so, Minter gave him a cheque to cover the cost of the distrained goods. . . .

Nothing more happened until the last week in August when Wacher demanded £101 for and on behalf of Margeretta Aylwin, and a few days later Minter was served with an eight day writ to appear in the High Court, King's Bench Division. Minter's lawyer got the case adjourned until the middle of October when another writ was issued, this time in the name of Frederick William Aylwin. The next day Minter drove into Canterbury and asked Charles Petley, the auctioneer, to conduct a farm sale for him at Michaelmas. He then saw Wacher and said that if he would give him a fair valuation for his Tenants' Rights at Goose Farm, he would accept as legal his Notice to Quit. Wacher replied "Custom of the country, custom of the country," and walked away.

Minter arranged for Holman Bros, Thrashing Machine Proprietors, to come in and thrash all his corn. He then wrote to Charles Petley telling him his services in the matter of a farm sale would not be required and engaged Mr E.L.Gardner of Castle Street, Canterbury, instead. After the corn had been threshed Minter hired a few square yards of George Mutton's market garden next door for a pound a year, and had the straw put on it, and then sold the stack to a friend from Deal. He sold his wheat to Kingsford's, his malting barley to Mackesons, engaging Baldock and his famous traction engine to deliver it. On the day of the sale Wacher appeared and gave Gardner notice in writing not to sell any Tenant's Rights and not to pay the sale proceeds to Minter until the action in the High Court had been settled

After the sale Minter got the money out of Gardner by cheque, which he banked. The bank manager told him that Wacher could garnishee the money and if Minter took it out in notes they could probably trace them. If, though, Minter took the notes to the Bank of England they would give him gold for them – which they did, tearing up the bank notes before his eyes as they did so

When Minter got back he found an old man called Budd in possession of the stack-yard at Goose Farm, placed there by a struggling auctioneer and valuer called Henry Meade Briggs. Next day, Minter came in from the fields to find Briggs inside the house shouting "No violence, no violence, I have got possession". He sent Budd for the Sturry policeman, Constable Woodgate, calling something after him. As Budd turned, Minter slammed the door behind him.

Briggs came back in different clothes the next day and on the pretext of having an important letter for him, persuaded Minter's old mother to open the window a little way, whereupon he forced a stout stick into the aperture and shouted "I have got possession".

Later that night Minter heard noises and found that they had taken the massive front door off its heavy rider and Briggs and Budd and a man called Thornby were struggling to carry it across the paddock to Thornby's cottage.

The next day three men with a push-truck containing ladders, four inch wide floorboards and carpenters' tools came in and began boarding up the windows. They were employed by the Sturry Building Company which had the offices in Mill Road later to be occupied by Mr Ernest Slingsby and then Mr H. R. French. (The firm is now only commemorated by name on some of the drain covers in Church Lane). There were seventeen windows at Goose Farm and the men only had enough material to board up half. Nobody else came near for three days except the postman, Charlie Clark. They tried to stop him getting to the farm but he said he was the Royal Mail and represented the Crown and thus could not be stopped by anyone at all.

About two o'clock the following Thursday Briggs brought up 28 young hooligans from Canterbury and Briggs' lady amused herself by driving past the farm again and again, putting her thumb to her nose and laughing immoderately until the men came and finished the boarding-up, locking Minter and his Mother into the house with padlocks. They also sent a man to block up the flue but he intentionally blocked up the flue to hirelings' room which Briggs and his men were using and had no connection with the house. Minter had a hammer indoors and so started knocking out one of the windows until Briggs caught the hammer and wrenched it out of his hand. Dr A. Godfrey Ince of Sturry said the tendons of Minter's arm were severely strained and the index finger fractured and the little finger dislocated at the middle joint.

On Monday, October 21st, smoke and other fumes started coming under the stone cill of the back door by means of a fumigating machine, the property of the Corporation of the City of Canterbury. Briggs said later that they were using a mixture of tar twine, cayenne pepper and other chemicals.

The men did this out of sight of the large crowd, hostile to the bailiffs, gathered at the front. Minter and his Mother had to keep close to the letter box in order to breathe. Just before one o'clock the police arrived: Superintendent Jacobs, Sergeant Wiseman and Constable Woodgate opened up the house and a distraint sale was held. Minter and his Mother came out, shook hands with Briggs, and, receiving a shout of welcome that could be heard in Canterbury, adjourned with the crowd to the Golden Lion.

Wacher re-let the farm to a man called Padgham who had married a Miss Terry and was the manager of the Sewage Farm in the Sturry Road, whence the smoke machine had come, John Pout and Mike O'Brien buying two lots at the sale. Padgham proved to be no farmer but made it pay by keeping pigs. The entire farm, together with Shelford farm was sold by auction on June 14th, 1919. A dairyman from Broad Street called Holness bought Goose Farm, which was later acquired by Mr E.J.Port from Margate.

A High Court action by Minter for damages against Wacher had a sad outcome for Minter. Mr Justice Grantham said they had to consider the conduct of Minter throughout the case, which he clearly didn't like, especially the selling off of the straw, and not paying his rent when he had gold in the house. Minter was described as "Fly, very fly," which the Judge didn't like either. The Judge said "The only question was, was an assault committed upon him, and, if so, what damages was he entitled to? Was there an assault committed by Briggs, and was the plaintiff damaged?" The jury found that there had been no assault and judgement entered for Wacher.

Arthur Minter was subsequently declared bankrupt and in 1910 went to New Zealand where he married the daughter of Sir Alfred Cadman. He never ceased to feel himself a victim of a grave injustice and in 1916 when the Germans started using poison gas against British troops in the trenches, (which was immediately declared against all international law), he wrote to the Prime Minister, Mr Asquith, in an unsuccessful attempt to get his case re-opened. He spent his later years in Deal, where he died a few days before his 81st birthday in 1952.

Abstracted from the account by Arthur Minter by courtesy of his son, Dr Alfred Minter.

The Annual Parish Dinner, 1910

by A.W.Minter

Arthur Minter had succeeded as Parish Councillor Adam Ingleton. Adam Ingleton was tenant of Godwin Farm and Britton Court, village carpenter, wheelwright, undertaker and was, as his father before him, landlord of The Golden Lion, where the Annual Parish Dinner was held each year.

It was a most enjoyable affair, about fifty sitting down to dinner. This was somewhat delayed by the late arrival of the Vicar, the Reverend H. Perry Brewer, who on these occasions was accorded first place. He was a splendid fellow, who was gifted with the happy knack of invariably doing the right thing at the right time and place. He would take the chair after dinner and before the fun became fast and furious he would diplomatically take his departure.

Mr Daniel Brice, a farmer at Buckwell Farm, aspired to County Council honours, and recognising the possibilities that might accrue through getting on a friendly footing with the electorate, did what he was never known to do before and attended the Parish Councillors' Dinner.

After the tables were cleared, punch was brought in (which Host Ingleton was a past master in the art of brewing) and other liquid refreshments, and the company settled down to an evening's enjoyment. When the Revd Mr Brewer vacated the Chair, by some means or other Daniel Brice secured it, although Robert Jezard was the Council Chairman at the time.

He thanked the company for the honour of electing him to the Chair (which they hadn't) and said he would do his best to give satisfaction. It was the first time he had attended one of these affairs and hoped it would not be the last, calling "Landlord, replenish the punch bowls" for which he received a tremendous ovation.

Some little time after, someone suggested that our worthy Chairman should give us a song. The Chairman rose and said "It's not much in my line, gentlemen, but I will do my best. We cannot sing or listen to a song with nothing to drink. Landlord, replenish the punch bowls". The company cheered to the echo but whether from the song or the punch, who can say?

He succeeded partly by singing and partly by reciting a very old hunting song, well-known in the vicinity. When the time was drawing near for the party to break up, the Chairman rose and said he wanted to say a few words in parting but "no man can listen to a speech without something to drink. Landlord, replenish the punch bowls," adding "and if any of you gentlemen would like something different, please give your orders."

While this was going on one old farmer said to another "I can't make Daniel out. I never knew him throw his money about like this before – three bowls at a time at ten or twelve shillings a bowl. . . . "

The Chairman said these gatherings conferred great benefit on the district by promoting friendly feelings. The company were quite in agreement for were there not living witnesses to this in the room that evening? To whit Jerry Hollands and Tom Studham. It appears that Jerry some time before had borrowed Tom's wheelbarrow and returned it without saying a word, broken.

When Tom had wanted to use this for a very special purpose, namely to assist his friend Jim Keen to get his wife home one Saturday night she having come over somewhat faint on coming out of the Royal Oak, this was his first intimation of the calamity. What made matters worse was that while Tom Studham was searching for another likely vehicle, an enterprising man in blue, namely Constable Woodgate, secured the services of a more up-to-date vehicle and drove poor Jim, as well as the sharer of his joys and sorrows, in an opposite direction to their home

Tom and Jerry were not on speaks for a time but after an hour or so an indefinable something seemed to thaw the icy coldness between them and they made up their differences, which affected them both so much they could not hold their tears back and when the loyal toast was given Jerry was asleep with his head on Tom's shoulder. He woke up though when their pal Fred Hall came with the punch ladle....

The Chairman announced that he was going to stand for the County Council at the next election in view of the great rise in our rates which he felt wanted looking into (cheers, with cries of "Good old Daniel") and in the course of time Daniel was duly elected. . . .

Seventhy Years Ago. . . .

Figures in connection with the Sturry housing scheme at Broad Oak were submitted by the Surveyor [to the Bridge Rural District Council]. He stated that if the Council decided not to agree to the special conditions, but to accept the subsidy of £3.15s. per house yearly he estimated the following rents would be necessary to make the scheme self-supporting.

If the special conditions were agreed to, and the subsidy of £7.10s per annum was accepted the estimated rents would be 6s 6d.., 5s. 3d., 7s 9d and 6s.6d. per week, respectively.

There was some discussion on the question of whether application should be made for the special subsidy, or whether it should be for the lower amount per house, with less onerous conditions. It was decided to put the scheme forward for the lower subsidy.

The Kentish Gazette, August 31st, 1931

Mains water pipes being laid opposite Dorinda Cottages, Shalloak Road, Broad Oak, in 1930.

Dalmally House and Broad Oak Lodge

At some unknown date towards the end of the nineteenth century a great house, then named Dalmally after a place in Scotland, was built on the brow of Shalloak Hill facing south in what was known as Peel's field. It was owned by Mr James E. Finch, whose family ran a wholesale confectionery and preserves business in North Lane, Canterbury, and later lived in Wellington House in St Stephen's Road (now the office of the Registrar of Births, Marriages and Deaths).

In 1900 he had two dwellings built at the bottom of the hill by the Shelford railway level crossing for his employees – they were called Dalmally Cottages and the date stone is still visible there. (The crossing-keeper at that time was called Baker and his cottage called the Blue House.) Mr Finch had wanted a large area of land in which to breed race horses and there are still some remains of buildings in a field next to the houses which were later built on the site which had probably been stables – he didn't train race horses, he just bred them.

After the purchase of this and the rest of the Sturry Court estate by Alfred, Lord Milner about 1904/5, the house became known as Broad Oak Lodge, the name used during the First World War when it was used as a Convalescent Hospital for Canadian soldiers. Occupants in the nineteen-twenties included Ernest Stennett and his family but at some time before 1937 when Jack Wood's family came to Shelford Farm it is known to have been derelict, perhaps because of subsidence. After the war it was demolished completely – many local boys admitting to have played in the ruins and assisted in its demolition – and a pair of fine semi-detached houses were built on the site, still known as Broad Oak Lodge.

Photograph by courtesy of Patsy Kerr

Looking north towards Lynne and Dengrove Woods and the site of Dalmally House during the Beating of the Bounds in 1910 led by William Lott (killed in action 7th October 1916). Stanley H.Jennings, later Mayor and Alderman of Canterbury City Council is fourth from the left, all with willow wands.

The First World War

Reprinted from the Sturry Parish Magazine for August, 1964

The village was a busy place in the days that followed the outbreak of the First World War on 4th August, 1914. The Ist East Kent Yeomanry arrived in Broad Oak and were billeted in the farms. We had 34 horses and the gun section at Goose Farm, and Mr Fleet at Hawe Farm, Mr Hatton at Sweech Farm, Mr George Matthews at Bramble Farm and Mr Maxted at Broad Oak Farm all had horses and men, too. The Sittingbourne Troop brought all their equipment in a traction engine and truck. The Margate Troop came by bus and the Canterbury Troop walked! The West Kents were camped first at Sturry Court and then at the top of Staines Hill – a place still known as the Camp, although now a K.C.C. depot. The East Kents were camped at the Polo Ground in the Littlebourne Road and the Surreys at the top of Fordwich Hill.

I have still got the poster called "Kent Defence" issued by the Home Division Emergency Committee for the Parish of Sturry telling people what to do in an invasion. Sturry folk were to go through Broad Oak to Mayton Farm, through Mayton Farm to Tyler Hill, Britton Court, Giles Lane and so on – via Bedlam Lane, Chart – to Cranbrook. They were only to be permitted to carry clothing, money and food – "all articles unnecessary for sustenance to be left behind".

Fortunately the village did not have to be evacuated and I suppose very few people ever realised that there had been plans for it in that war. I think that Sarre and St Nicholas were the nearest places that Zeppelins dropped incendiaries in those days.

Edward J.Port

Royal East Kent Mounted Rifles at Hawe Farm, Popes Lane, November 1914.

Carol, Hope, Winifred, Barbara and Bertram Headley at Hawcroft Farmhouse, Hawe lane, 1934. (Demolished in the 1970's)

Photograph by courtesy of Jan Gaskell

At Dengrove Cottages, by Broad Oak Lodge. Annie, Bert Pritchard,Henry, Arthur, George, Mercy and Daisy (Ginny)Pritchard

Broad Oak Lodge in World War I

By Hazel Basford

In the First World War Broad Oak Lodge became a privately run convalescent home for officers. The property, since demolished, belonged to Lord Milner, then Secretary of State for War. The expenses were paid by Lady Julia Drummond, the wife of Sir George Drummond. She worked at the London Headquarters of the Canadian Red Cross, where she also financed a department of information on the wounded and missing. Her son, Lieutenant Guy Melfort Drummond, had died on 22nd April 1915 at the age of 27.

The Commandant was Mrs Alice Yates, the widow of Lt-Colonel Yates also of Montreal, who had a staff of four VAD nurses, including one who was a trained nurse and another with nursing experience, and kitchen help. The hospital, which opened in 1917, had ten beds, medical assistance being available at the Granville at Ramsgate and the Canterbury Military Hospital. (This hospital, sited roughly where the Crown Court now is, was demolished in the nineteen twenties.

A report of 28th March 1917 by a Captain in the Canadian Divisional Engineers stated that there were two bathrooms and that all the plumbing was in good order. (1) He noted "that there is a splendid supply of water, both hot and cold, the water being obtained by pumping from a well into an overhead reservoir from where it is distributed by gravity, the water is pure but hard. There is not gas or electric light, the premises being lit by candles and oil lamps. The site is healthy one. The rooms are airy and light and have ample ventilation….the sewage is in perfect order."

(1) Canadian Archives (RG 9 III BI Vol 3416, H-26-47, Hospital Accommodation File.)

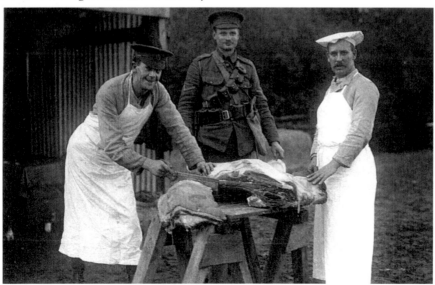

Photograph by courtesy of Jan Gaskell

Army butchers at Broad Oak in World War I

Sweech Farm
Diary, 1917-1919

This diary, interleaved with blotting paper, kept by Charles A. Hatton of Sweech Farm and bought at a boot fair. It relates solely to the work carried out daily by the farmer and his farm worker, referred to only as Ned. It records a farming year very different from that of today, the killing of pigs, both his own and those belonging to other people, being a frequent occurrence. The various activities concerned with wood – cutting whithies, making wattles, sawing wood for faggots and mending hurdles - being another occupation.

Many days were spent spuddling wurtzels (sic). A spuddle was a form of broad share fitted to an old Kent plough – a single leg with a frog with a point doing work that would be done today by a cultivator in hours rather than days. Filling a dung cart and spreading the contents was another time-consuming occupation as was seasoning wheat, seasoning being the preparation of the seed bed for sowing. The carring or carrying of wheat was the taking of wagon loads of sheaves for stacking.

The finances of yesteryear are difficult to relate to today's values. Thirteen hours of gardening were done for someone called Bellman who paid six shillings and sixpence for it. Ned, the farm –worker, was paid £1.4 s 3 d per week in 1917. By 1919 his wages had risen to £1.13s 3d per week. Cutting hay led to nine hours overtime one week for Ned who was paid at 7d per hour – a total of five shillings and three pence. Hiring two horses from Fuller for ten hours at 2/- per hour cost the farmer £1.

And Boxing Day was not a Bank Holiday – Charles Hatton and Ned spent it cutting turnips.

Nelson Bubb

Photograph by courtesy of Mike Guiby

The Thatch Chapel Lane after the fire and before reconstruction

Photograph by Robin Q Edmonds

Brookside
By Hazel Basford

The house known as Brookside in Mayton Lane, is one of the most interesting and unusual in Broad Oak. Attached to it when it was first built were eighteen acres of agricultural land still known as "Council Land". Erected sometime in late 1919 or early 1920 the house is in the style made famous by the architect Sir Edwin Lutyens. It was part of a post First World War resettlement scheme for returning soldiers organised by the Board of Agriculture.

This was first proposed locally by the Ministry of Labour in January, 1919, when Captain Johnson of the Appointments Department of the Ministry addressed the Canterbury Farmers' Club on the subject of the employment of officers in agriculture. Following this a Committee was established by the Kent County Council in February 1919 to take the scheme forward, the costs being borne by the State and no charge to fall on local rates until March 31, 1925.

By 31st May 1919 ex-servicemen and women who desired to settle on the land had been invited to apply, the Land Settlement (Facilities) Act having been passed and 488 acres of land in Kent having been bought for this purpose by the Kent County Council, as reported in The Times for 22nd May, 1919 under the heading "Land for Soldiers in Kent". In spite of a diligent search of local records it has not been possible to identify the first occupants with any certainty, although the name of Coppins has been mentioned.

Brookside, Mayton Lane, Broad Oak, in April, 2001

Photograph by Paul Crampton

Village Voices - 2

An edited extract of an interview with Bob and Betty Murphy by Heather Stennett in 2001

Bob   What sort of things do you want to know about?

Heather   First of all your names and how long you've lived in the Village

Betty   Oh, right. Well, I'm Betty Murphy and I was Betty Keem and I was born in 1941 along Sweechgate Cottages and I have lived here all my life. I went to school at Sturry, All the usual things.

Heather   How many were in your family, Betty?

Betty   Three girls, three boys – my brother Tony was the first baby to be born in Sweechgate Cottages. I'm the youngest of a large family. A bit cramped but enjoyable, as all the houses were along there. There wasn't an awful lot of room in any of them. I thought that everyone had a particularly happy childhood along there. I can remember it was before cars, because I can remember playing hopscotch in the road and on the Pout Oast, the part that was left. I remember playing ball on there and very rarely did we have to get out of the way for a car or anything coming along there. Of course there was no houses on the left of the village there, apart from one or two. There was Mrs Scott lived along there, didn't she, and the Collingwoods? And Mrs [Agnes] Pout and old Mrs [Charlotte] File. Other than that it was just council houses on the right. So it was quite a small village then.

Heather   What did your father do for a living

Betty   He worked for Bretts on the quarries – as far as I know I think that was the only job he ever had. He was also a gamekeeper actually, spare time. He had the shoot at most of the woods and also he used to go fishing down in the lakes. So although we was crowded and very poor we lived quite well because we had everything that he brought home. There was usually plenty of rabbits and I can remember

him bringing home small Hessian sacks with the eels in, still alive, that he would actually kill in the sink and I used to love these, but I mean if somebody offered me an eel now to eat, I couldn't eat it, but I know they were absolutely delicious, because he would actually kill them and skin them [spitchcock] and they would be chopped up and put straight in the frying pan, and I can remember that we sort of couldn't wait for these eels because it looked like they were flying, because when you put them in it looked as though they were jumping about. I can always remember that. But we lived very well, really. I can't say that we ever went hungry. We didn't have things like butter, and if you had marg on your bread, then you didn't have jam and things like that. I suppose it was quite frugal really, but my Mum was an excellent cook and she seemed to make things out of nothing, like a lot of women did then, and I know that when my Mum died and I had to take over from her when I was about sixteen or seventeen, I found it terribly difficult to manage how she'd managed because she was just excellent at making ends meet as we all had sort of enough. I suppose we were quite lucky, as I said, in that my father had the shoot of most of the woods around here. He was quite a good, well, countryman really. He did net and shoot rabbits and fish and so he did quite well.

Heather   Did your mother go out to work? Like seasonal work?

Betty   Yes, oh yes, definitely, yes, seasonal work. I don't know how she had the time to do it really, when you think how busy they were. But it was very enjoyable and of course, my brother-in-law, Ron and my elder sister, Nora, they had the village shop, which was in front of the Royal Oak, because Ron's mother Mrs [Lily] Birch, had the pub. It was a general stores which was like a butchers, a grocery and a greengrocery. And it was a very busy shop, actually. I remember having to work most Saturdays delivering things and in the summer I remember the highlight of Gillian [Birch] and my week was the day that we went up to Mrs

Tharp's, right at the top of Mayton, and Ron used to load the trades bike up with these two huge boxes of groceries and we used to walk up there and I know I used to think that as wonderful. There was always a bag of sweets on the top of the boxes for us to eat going and coming back. That really sticks in my mind.

Heather   There were two other shops, weren't there, as well?

Betty   Yes, there was, we used to call it "Albert's", [Sweechgate Stores] that's the Post Office, and that used to fascinate me in there because he sold absolutely everything. We used to even get our plimsolls in there for school, you know, it was one of the really old-fashioned shops and it was quite fascinating. And then I can't remember the other, when there was a Post Office at this end.

Heather   Shrubbery Stores - The Ords and Mrs Fullagar.

Betty   Oh, yes. The Ords used to live in Tharp's Cottages next to the Whitings. Old Mr Whiting used to be the local roadman with his little old barrow, he used to go round and do everything. He was wonderful. Keep the roadways clean and do everything. And you could see this barrow there and nobody would touch it. You can't do that today, can you?

Heather   No

Bob   But I go back before that. I was born in 1932 and I remember going to Milner Court when I was very young to – what do you call it? A coronation or something like that in the Thirties.

Heather   Possibly in 1937

Bob   They had a big do there and I remember going up and getting a little prize, but apart from that I remember the war starting and the day war started we all came out and everyone was talking and so on, and the ice-cream man came along with his little old bike and everything was half price. I thought that was wonderful, you know, and so we all had an ice-ream to celebrate the war starting, I suppose. Going on about the war, Brook's Farm was full of troops and also Milner Court. And they had the hut as their cookhouse so they used to come up here and have their meals and outside the hut was an apple tree of some sort. I wonder whether it's still there. Is it in the corner?

Heather No

Bob As boys we used to camp at the farm. And when the army would be in there having their food and they'd bring us their sweet out, you know, apple pie, whatever they were having, wonderful. I remember where you lived, Heather, there was three, just by the sign, three bombs dropped in there that didn't go off and one dropped in Mark Holmes' garden at the time, but there has been a house built there since. The other side of the road, right on the corner, as you go the alley way, a bomb dropped in there and it bounced and went off over in the field. And they evacuated from about Topsy [Moran]'s house right along your Gran's house and everybody went up to Hoath School for several days until they got the bombs out. I suppose you knew that, though, didn't you?

Heather I have heard some tales about it.

Bob Another thing happened at school. We used to do half a day up at the Hut. They all decided that if a bomb dropped on the school or something they'd lose everybody, so they started pushing the children out and then half a day in the Hut for a period there and they could go home for the rest of the day. Or, if we was at school we would be most of the time in the shelter. It was some wonder we learnt anything, really.

Heather Did you know anything about the day when the landmines dropped on Sturry?

Bob Yes, I remember that. It was great because all the buses and everything came round through Broad Oak for about a week. Couldn't get through [Sturry]. Of course, being kids we couldn't care less about Sturry, although one of my friends was killed in Sturry, who went to school with us. And then there was [Charles F.] Cork

and that who had shops in Sturry. All their sweets and that was brought up to the corner of Popes Lane and all stacked up. So we was over there, getting all these sweets, being warned by everybody that they would be contaminated or something but it didn't matter, you know. Free sweets for some time. Then they build a reservoir thing there in concrete for incendiary bombs and things like that. There was a man lived over at Port's, I can't remember his name now [Walter Strand] but he was in a bus coming along Sturry Road – he got killed, didn't he?

Heather Yes, my grandmother was a passenger on that bus.

Betty It was with a machine gun, wasn't it?

Bob Yes, from aircraft. And I remember your uncle being killed, Heather, at Arnhem, wasn't it? Bill. Bill Bacon.

Heather Certainly he was. It was a parachute drop.

Bob And he was a boxer. Everybody admired him, you know. Yes, so the war really had a great impact one way or another on my generation, didn't it?

Heather Well, it must have affected your schooling, I would have thought.

Bob It must have done. I mean, we didn't have proper teachers. We had some of the older ones but most of them had gone to the war like Mr [Thomas] Blake and Mr [Eric F] Hyde and Mr [Ronald] Ratledge. So we had whoever they could get. I mean, one

chap in particular, Mr Hill, he was a brilliant musician and he used to come and teach. Well, I knew more about maths than he did at the time, and I was his star pupil. Poor old chap. But he was a smashing bloke, you know. But I mean it wasn't happening, was it? It held you back a bit, didn't it? But it was a lovely class really.

Heather Did you have an air-raid shelter at home?

Bob Yes. Well, we had a Morrison. Bet's family had an Anderson. That's an outside one. We had a Morrison, it was inside and my old Grandfather used to come up and he'd sleep in there and if there was a raid then there used to be a terrific noise from these raids round here, we'd run down and jump in on him. Oh, he used to crack on. Well, Father would go out as a Home Guard, you know, and he'd go out not knowing whether we would jump in on the old fellow.

Heather It was like a reinforced table, was it, the Morrison?

Bob Yes, a table, with mesh all round, and a reinforced top, middle and sides. In the front room. It was quite big and bolted together. You couldn't lift it.

Heather And Betty you had an Anderson?

Betty Yes, that's right. It was sort of all covered in earth and you just went down steps into it. There was only room for us without any furniture.

Bob They had a load of what they called Bertha guns that used to run up and down the road firing at planes. And the noise they made was incredible. A lot of the ceilings and that came down

Change of Address 1920's style

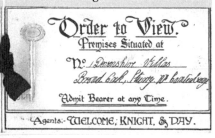

because of the guns – one of ours did. There was a big hole there. Mr Atkins said that that's what happened.

Heather   A lot of the families I've spoken to – and my own Mother – said in the end they didn't get up and go to the shelters because they would rather stay in their own beds – they got so tired.

Betty   That's right.

Heather   Bet, can you describe the kitchen in your house?

Betty   Yes, vividly, because I used to have to clean it! We had a range and it was my job to polish this blessed thing every Saturday morning with grate polish. It was black and came in a tin.

Heather   Zeebright?

Betty   Zeebright. That's right. We had the gas cooker range which my Mum cooked on but that was really much later. We had a sink with a curtain at the bottom of it. We had two armchairs by the range and a dresser and a table, a long table, with all the chairs round, and that's all there was room for in there. And then we had an outside loo – and it was only emptied once a week. It was dreadful really, you know, and towards the end of the time for them to come round and empty it, it was all pretty, sort of not very nice.

Bob   What an awful job to do it, though. The stink used to be terrible, didn't it?

Betty   Oh, yes. We used to hate the day that men came with this great big sort of tanker. It was like a big round lorry, wasn't it, and the village used to smell terrible. It was an absolute wonder to us when they actually came through and put bathrooms in the council houses. That was amazing for us because we used to bath once a week in a big cottage bath in front of the fire, and because I was the youngest one I was allowed to go in first and then all the others gone in after me.

Bob   We didn't have electrics until the Fifties.

Betty   No, and I think we were later than you having electric. I think my Dad stood out against it and we didn't have electric until quite late.

Bob   And we used to read of a night by candlelight, two or three candles. The good old days!

Betty   And then you'd hear the gas mantles pop and you'd have to run up to the shop to get a new one and put it back.

Bob   We had blackouts in the war, didn't we, when you only had gas or candlepower. I think it was Mr Chaplin that used to go around shouting to everything about that. And your Dad was the local policeman in the war.

Betty   P.C. Keem, Special Constable, with   Sergeant   Street. Didn't he confiscate your catapult one day?

Bob   Yes, he did. You see us boys, well it was all in the war, we were all big ramblers. Every weekend we used to go up in the woods early in the morning until late afternoon, war or not, rabbitting and squirrelling, you see. Along comes P.C.Keem and he took all the catapults.

Heather   So you're talking about your mates. How many boys of your age would have been in your gang?

Bob   Anything up to ten or a dozen. Your parents wouldn't worry about you and you'd be away all day

Heather   Did you ever play down by the brook?

Betty   The whole summer. There used to be whole crowds of us down there and we used to swim in the brook and catch the little red-finned fish in there.

Bob   This gang of ours, we all learnt to swim down the brook just past old Lloydie's [Stanley George Lloyd] at the bottom of Calcott Hill. About half a mile down we damned it. You see, we had a Molotov breadbasket, well half a one. When the Germans dropped this breadbasket, it was a great big shell at the bottom and it came open and all the incendiaries would come out. Well, it was ideal for a boat, these arc things so we led one down there and we used to go up and down with these as a boat. We couldn't get to the beach at Herne Bay then or anywhere because it was all wired off so we made our own arrangements.

Heather   Well done.

Bob   And I know Lloydie used to chase us occasionally because we used to have a cook-up down there, get the old fire going. He had a smallholding there so we used to creep off up there and get a few onions and carrots and things and God, he used to get wild. He had a job to – well, he couldn't catch us, but it was quite novel for him to come down there. But he chased us right up through the woods to Ron's on occasions. But we used to get back again. We didn't have a lot, just a handful of onions and things. I can remember a couple of planes coming down when I was up at Mayton.

[at 1.35 p.m. on Sunday, August 18th 1940 a Hawker Hurricane (P3208) from No. 501 Squadron, Gravesend, crashed on Calcott Hill, resulting in the death of Pilot Officer John Wellburn Bland. Later in the Battle for Britain a Spitfire came down on Blaxland Farm land, the pilot surviving. It came in very low, just clearing the brook before crashing about fifty yards from the stream on the right and was soon being guarded by the army. Les Moran, then a ten-year-old schoolboy, was allowed by the soldiers to clamber into the cockpit.]

Bob   Another very funny thing was when the balloons from Canterbury used to break loose and if there was a wind invariably they used to come over here. So, we'd seen them go down and come and cut all the ropes off them. One day one came down at Fox Hill, just inside the wood. The police constable, he knew it was there, but by the time he had got down there, we had got all the ropes. Well, he couldn't find it. We'd stripped these lumps of balloon out by the time he'd found it. Well, we told him where it was but when he turns up we'd stripped it.

Heather   So you used to take trophies if you could, then ?

Bob   Well, we used to use the bits of the balloons as tents and things, you know. And the ropes we would often put up in the woods as swings and things like that.

Heather   So why were the balloons hanging over Canterbury?

Bob   They were all round Canterbury to protect it against the planes coming too low. It didn't work.

Heather Then there was an aircraft down on Fox Hill. . .

Bob It was a Dornier, they say. It was a great big aircraft. I thought it was going to hit the council houses but it just went over the top and came down in the wood. And none of them bailed out, these Germans, and they were all dead apparently.

[At 12.40 p.m. on Sunday, September 15th, 1940, Dornier Do 172-3, 2651, of Unit 3/KG76, crashed in flames and exploded in trees at Hawcroft Farm. All four occupants were killed. They were buried first in Sturry Cemetery, and later reinterred at the German War Cemetery at Cannock Chase.]

Bob Then I used to go long-netting with my uncle Ted Beecham. He used to rabbit professionally for the railway. That was his job. He used to go along the tracks, keeping the rabbits under. Do you know about long-netting? You put a net up and go right round, go round in the wind so the rabbits can't smell you - once the nets are up let them smell you and they run into the net.

Heather Were there any prisoners-of-war round here?

Bob Yes, up at Trenley Park on Fordwich Hill and then when we were young, we used to go up and play football. Always used to beat us, though. Brilliant footballers. We was only old boys. There was a lot of verbal abuse going on and they was ever so good. They enjoyed it and so did we. Nearly every Sunday we went up there. Bert Williams used to get a team up. He was a good footballer, was Bert.

Heather Can you remember the picture shows that used to be on in the village hall

Betty I can vaguely remember them, yes.

Bob But Sheila [Keem] was on the committee and we called her "Miss Committee" and we used to go over the pub and get all tanked up and go over there at half past ten and she made us pay full fare to get in. She was always a row, but she wouldn't let us in until we had paid the lot, and we was only there perhaps for three quarters of an hour or something. Liven the place up.

Betty Yes, it was quite peaceful until they all arrived.

Bob It used to be dead until we got over there

Heather What did they do – play records or was there a band?

Bob Records. Occasionally there was a band on there, but mainly records. Old Time ones.

Heather I can just remember when they were still having socials there. And all the village seemed to go.

Bob Everyone was asked.

Betty It wasn't an invitation. If a local person got married, then in the evening everyone went.

Heather Tell me about the mushrooms. Wild mushrooms.

Bob Old Mr [Donald] Sweeting [M.P.S.] lived at Mead Manor and was a chemist and he told us which mushrooms we could eat.

Betty We always used to go and pick them. I remember when we were very young we used to go out into Lawrence's fields and pick mushrooms, and when we went Bramley apple picking up the drove, we always got the mushrooms up there.

Bob Of course in those days they didn't have sprays, did they? You just had to watch them for maggots

Betty I think you can always tell ordinary field mushrooms. It's getting a bit dicey, though, when you start getting them really coloured ones and shaped ones. But we always used to pick mushrooms. . . .

Monkey Island

Many older local residents have reported that once upon a time it was customary for conductors on the old East Kent Road Car Company's buses to call out "Monkey Island" when the stop at Sweechgate was reached. It has proved impossible to find any other than oral evidence of this, although the late Frank J. Neaves, who was born at Langton Lodge in 1911, knew that a dead monkey had been buried in a field near his home there. It was in fact the pet monkey belonging to T.Sidney Cooper's wife, Margaret, that had its own rather ornate grave - since demolished - at Mayton Farm, and recorded by Brian Stewart in his book THOMAS SIDNEY COOPER OF CANTERBURY, (Meresborough Books, 1983). Maurice Collingwood thought the use of these words might have originated with his uncle, George Allen of Applegarth, as he used the expression all the time.

Broad Oak in Fiction

The detective story IN THE DEAD OF THE NIGHT by the prolific author, Harry Carmichael (Collins, 1956), is set in an imaginary house called Summerhill in the real village of Sturry. Situated at a place he named High Felstead on the road to Herne Bay, the area described is clearly halfway up the east side of Calcott Hill, the plot involving, among others, a cautious Scottish doctor.

Operation Overlord – June 6th, 1944

It was a well-established military ploy to try to make Adolf Hitler believe that the D-Day Landings in Normandy were merely a feint for the real attack that was going to made on the Pas de Calais.

On the morning of the D-Day landings Arthur Epps, while serving customers at Sweechgate Stores, waved to a sergeant in a tank that rumbled by. An hour later he waved to the same sergeant in the same tank – and so on throughout the day – when he realised that he was in effect watching a stage army. It was Normandy that was for real after all.

VE Day Celebrations outside Sweechgate Cottages, with Mr Robert Collingwood on right. Among others present were members of the Moran, Birch, Tomlin, Jackman, Dale, Baker, Keem, Webb, Ward, Yeoman, Kennett, Beecham, Chaplin, Hall, Todd, Gammon, Jordan, Holmes, Mayo, Twyman, Blackman, Jones, and Roy families.

Sweechgate Stores in 1955, the Thompson twins, Elizabeth and Brian, in the pram

Farming in Broad Oak

By Linda Lodge (née Thompson)

"A farmer should live as though he was going to die tomorrow, but he should farm as though he was going to live forever".

The process of cutting down trees and growing crops began with our neolithic ancestors and continued through the centuries with Roman and Germanic settlers extending the land cultivated beyond the dry, easily-worked soils favoured by pre-historic man to the richer and heavier land covered by natural forest.

Blean Woods, which form the northern boundary of Broad Oak, are all that remains of an extensive forest but the heavy clay soil has guaranteed its continued existence. Even in the sixteenth century there were still large areas of woodland, including much of the Sarre Penn valley. The later clearance only became economically viable with the prosperity of agriculture in the seventeenth and eighteenth centuries.

The timber trade was another element of farming in the parish with chestnut trees coppiced every fifteen years and used for fencing. Ash provided the long straight poles necessary for tool handles and timber for the wheelwrights. The mature oaks were felled for building and horse-drawn timber wagons moving up and down Mayton Lane would have been a common sight for several hundred years. Woodcutters, carpenters and wheelwrights were still prominent in the 1901 village census.

Land-holdings were much smaller than those today. Mayton farm, for instance, comprised only 74 acres of farmable land in 1640, and this was divided among three tenants. By 1850 it was owned by Michael Bass of the Burton-on-Trent brewing family and was reputed to have grown a hundred acres of hops. A four

kiln oast house remains, now with the cowls removed. In 1875 the farm was acquired by the renowned local artist, Thomas Sidney Cooper, which together with the adjoining land at Brambles Farm, became part of the Little Hall estate.

Vale Farm latterly comprised one hundred and twenty acres but in the days of George Laslett who worked it from 1813 until his death in 1853, its acreage was 218. Hops were grown here, too, as was wheat, with an average growth per acre of 32 quarters, using a

Kentish turn-wrest plough, a plough so heavy that it could only be pulled by a four-horse team.

Goose Farm had 76 acres of arable and pasture land, having formerly been part of the Shelford estate. It was bought by Edward J. Port of Margate just before the 1st World War and was still owned by the family until the death of his son, Edward (Teddy) O. Port in 1979. Sweech Farm was acquired by the Lawrence family in 1921.

In the 1901 census almost the entire population of Broad Oak was employed in agriculture either working on the land as a labourer, waggoner, cow-man or providing a service to the farming fraternity with blacksmiths, wheelwrights and so forth. Even the landlord of The Golden Lion describes his trade as licensed victualler and farmer, while Laythorne Blackman, the grocer, lists himself as baker and butcher, probably sourcing his meat direct from the farmer and slaughtering it himself. The daughters of many of the labourers worked in the farmhouses. It was 1908 before the State Pension of 5/-per week was introduced and it was common to find men still working at an

Photograph by courtesy of Linda Thompson

THE SUMMER GANG Including Molly Rose, Lily Milliner, Jane Murphy, Frank Wells, Ivy Macey, Dolly Fallon, Ella Gammon, Marjorie Maidment, Rose Chaplin, Eileen Brown, Joyce Giles, Beatrice Baldock, Agnes Gisby, Peggy Chaplin, Kath Thompson and Kathleen Fairbrass.

advanced age. Thomas Kemp was still working as a farm labourer at the age of 73 years. The migratory nature of farm workers is evident in the many different parishes in which each succeeding child in the family is registered.

Broad Oak Farm where my father, Bill, worked was a large fruit farm owned by Mr P.T.S.Brook. Fruit growing in the 1950's was very labour-intensive and both men and women were employed throughout the year. My father's diaries record pruning, grafting, spraying and harvesting. The women, including my mother, Kath, were mainly employed to thin the blossom and then the fruit in the apple orchards before picking, grading and packing in the summer and autumn.

Mr Brook had the foresight to have a reservoir built in the early 1960s. This had a capacity of 4 and a half million gallons and water for it was pumped up from the Sarre Penn during the winter months for irrigating the orchards in the spring and summer. As will be seen, my father records varieties of fruit which have long since disappeared from shops and supermarkets. He notes the location of every job of work by referring to the local names of field and orchards such as Jock's Piece, Brooder Piece, Macey's Miller's, etc.

Today Broad Oak Farm is owned by Mansfield's and most of the families in the local farmhouses do not farm and there are no hops grown in the parish any longer. And those temporary workers who now pick the fruit will not be aware that they are picking Bramleys on Mayton bank, strawberries at Shelford or pears in Birch's Piece. They will pick apples, too, in Wyman's field where just over half a century ago my father found the flint tool which had begun to shape the farming tradition that survived, albeit much changed, to the twenty-first century in Broad Oak.

Photograph by Jean Smith

P.T.S.Brook and Ted Bubb at Broad Oak Farm

Photograph by courtesy of Derek Butler

Edward O. Port of Goose Farm, Broad Oak, posing by his lorry during the picking of cabbages in the savage winter of 1946/7. Others there include Fred Atkins, Jim(Bunge) Keem and MacDonald Milliner.

A Year with Fruit

The great importance of the weather and its effect on his day's work is very evident in the diary kept for the year 1951 by the late Bill Thompson of 1, The Bungalow, next to Yew Tree Cottage, Shalloak Road, Broad Oak, who worked for P.T.S.Brook at Broad Oak Farm. It is a fascinating account of the fruit farm's annual round of pruning, spraying (usually referred to as washing), grafting, thinning and harvesting. Fields were often called "pieces".

The year's work began on New Year's Day (not a Bank Holiday then) with the pruning of the young Cox's apples, then the [Lord] Derby and Cox's. [In an orchard of Derby's every third tree was a Cox tree planted for pollination purposes.] This followed by the digging of trenches for blackcurrants –a six of them, thirty feet long and eighteen inches deep – on a day made memorable for him by the finding of "a good example of a Stone Age flint".

Winter washing with Mortegg came next, then pruning the Beauty of Bath apples and the spraying of pears and currants and Warwickshire Drooper plums. Planting up gaps in currants was another January task as were fixing wires for the Lloyd George raspberries and spraying Victoria and Belle de Louvain plums. He noted that it rained sixteen days out of thirty-one that month. [Lloyd George raspberries had been found by J.J.Kettle as a seedling growing in a wood in Kent. He took the variety with him when he settled in Corfe Mullen in Dorset and introduced it in 1919.]

Photograph by courtesy of Maurice Collingwood

Annie Collingwood outside her home at Sweechgate on Coronation Day, June 6th, 1953.

Photograph by courtesy of Ellen Lake

On the way to the Coronation celebrations in the Royal Oak field, 2nd June, 1953 with Albert Hadlow as the nurse. Also in the picture are Mr and Mrs Ernest Kemp, Mrs Mabel Dunn, George Tomlin, Sybil Jakeman, Jean Webb, and Pat Raine.

Pruning in Slip [maiden] Cox's and then Old Cox's and Big Cox's took up much of February as did grafting as well as washing the Miller's Seedlings and Bramleys. At that time it was the wettest February on record for fifty-one years.

March began with the washing of Worcesters and the cutting off of the tops of the [Lord] Derbys for grafting. The pruning of blackcurrants and the sorting of potatoes followed, with a special note being made on Monday, 19th March, of the installation of an automatic telephone in the Broad Oak box. The Early Victoria apples were prepared for grafting, followed by the Tydemans. It rained on sixteen days in March.

Lime and sulphur washing of the Mendip currants started in April as did the planting of Arran Pilot and Eclipse potatoes. Rain fell in twelve days. He then sprayed four cants of Old Cox's, (cant being a word, used mainly in coppicing, for an area measure and also the fifty-yard length of the hoses supplying water to the fruit trees). May meant the hoeing of young pears and a trip to Brentford market, arriving there at 4.0 a.m. and reaching home by 9.0 a.m. Picking up broccoli was the next day's job and then hoeing the Laxton [Superb]s and washing the Worcester [Pearmain]s and the [Lord] Derbys. A less usual job was the unloading of 8 or 9 tons of feeding potatoes at the coal yard in Sturry between 8.0 a.m and 1 p.m. It was the coldest Whit Monday for thirty-five years although it only rained on ten days in May.

The June weather was good – rain on only seven days - and the jobs routine, including the riddling of potatoes, using liquid Derris for Red Spider, the picking of gooseberries and the hoeing of mangel-wurzels. National Service was having an impact and the names of some of those in the village being called up were noted.

July was hot – the Miller's Seedlings and Early Victoria apples had to be thinned in a temperature of just on 90 degrees – but work was interrupted by Bill Thompson being knocked off his bicycle and quite seriously injured and weather records were not kept for some time. He had recovered enough by September after weeks of hospital treatment to be taken to the South Bank Festival in London and was especially impressed by the opportunity to get inside a Lancaster bomber ("Good show") and four days later by the sight of the first Sabre jets he saw flying in Kent.

He resumed work still feeling shaky. Picking Laxton [Superb] apples and Wyndale plums then Bramleys and [Lord] Derbys – the crops being measured in bushels – were the first jobs he did. He recorded seeing the Northern Lights at 7.30 p.m. on October 28th. Pruning Old Cox's and Worcester [Pearmain]s came next, the fruit farming year drawing to a close in November with the cutting down of currants although "They were very badly off for young wood".

On November 10th he went to a Social organised by the Golden Lion Sports Club - "a good evening" and on December 3rd to the Friars Cinema to see "World's Collide" ("Not bad") . There had been rain on twenty consecutive days in November.

The Royal Oak Stores
By Mike Gisby

The Royal Oak Stores served the villagers for many years until the early 1960's. The shop itself, situated on the forecourt of the Royal Oak public house, was demolished in 1962. The store was run by Ron Birch and his wife Nora (nee Keem). Ron's mother, Mrs Lily Birch, was the licensee of the Royal Oak. The shop sold sweets and tobacco through the door to the left – the one to the right led to the butcher's department. You could also buy paraffin and chopped firewood and outside there was always a selection of fresh vegetables. If you wanted to, you could order your groceries and Ron would deliver them to your door on his trades bike, which can be seen in the photograph standing to the right of the shop.

The shop was greatly missed by the people of the village when it closed down.

Ron and Nora Birch's shop in front of The Royal Oak

Photograph by Mike Gisby

The Man in White

In the winter of 1950, Dr R.A.C.McIntosh, the recent proud possessor of a brand-new green Rover car, (new cars were a rarity then), delivered by the light of an oil-lamp a son to the family living in the house by the level crossing, opposite Dalmally Villas at Shelford. (It had been built in Frank Cooper's time for the foreman at Shelford Farm and is now derelict). Unlike the lighting in the house, the car was the latest word in electrical advances in that it was one of the very first vehicles designed to have a courtesy light that came on when the car door was opened.

After the delivery the doctor came out of the house intending to have a quiet smoke – even doctors smoked then – before returning to make sure that the new mother was all right. He was gowned from head to toe in white, with a white cap on his head and was wearing a white mask. As he opened the car door this faceless white figure was illuminated by the new-fangled courtesy light. From somewhere nearby he heard a scream and much enjoyed listening to later rumours of a ghost having been seen thereabouts.

Photograph by courtesy of Mrs Ellen Luke

Jack Collard of Nook Farm, Mayton Lane, in the early nineteen-fifties, one of the last thatchers in the county.

A Farmer's Tale

Edited extract of an interview of Jack Wood by Heather Stennett in 2001

Heather   Can I ask you your association with this area?

Jack   My family goes back to 1712 at Blean but in 1937 my father bought Shelford Farm from the Executors of Frank Cooper who had had it since 1919. He had the Hanging Banks sandpit off the Broad Oak Road and another one up Shalloak Hill and set up a brickworks for making sand/lime bricks, putting in a foreman at the farm. It was a much bigger farm in days gone by. There were the remains of the Manor House there then – it had been one of Sir Roger Manwood's manors – but it was in a pretty derelict state having been used by troops in the war.

Heather   That would be the First World War?

Jack   That was the First World War and in 1919 when Frank Cooper took it over, not wanting to live there, he pulled it down and built a couple of bungalows recovered from the demolition of the old house. So then in 1937 my father bought it and we moved there. We came across foundations and the well, and the remains of a croquet lawn with a pond in the corner and wych elms and a privet hedge and a kitchen garden with old fruit trees – greengages, Victoria plums. And an oast – there was an oast on most farms then. Obviously it was bought on a mortgage. My father had a bad heart and so was uninsurable and he had got a mortgage of £1000 which was a lot of money in those days and in 1942 when I was 18 I wanted to go to war. My father said that if I wanted to volunteer and go away to war, he was going to sell the farm because he couldn't allow the prospect of my mother, who wasn't a business-woman, being left alone because aircrews' lives were not very lengthy in those days.

Heather   What type of farming did you do?

Jack   Well, basically we were there a long time so our farming pattern changed. But from the time we came here until 1965 dairy herds were the basis of the farm. My father bought a dairy herd here when he first came and when he took over running Folly Farm next door, [now only accessible from the far end of Headcorn Drive, Canterbury,] in 1947 he established another dairy herd there, although they were later combined into one. In addition we grew cereals. We grew quite a lot of vegetables and my father used to take them to shops in Canterbury. What are termed in the trade "rough vegetables" . . . .

Heather   Rough vegetables?

Jack   Swede turnips, cabbages, Brussels sprouts, potatoes – that sort of thing. Not the more exotic Spring onions and carrots and that sort of thing. When we took over Folly it had thirty acres of fruit so we were growing fruit. By the way, I didn't go to war. They wouldn't take me, which is another thing. And in 1947 my father said I ought to know something about sheep so we established a flock of Kent sheep and we ran those for quite a number of years. And we had Ayrshire cattle and grew cereals and some seed productions so it was a truly mixed farm which a generation or so ago was the thing to do. In these days it's the very last thing that one does.

Heather   How many people were employed at the farm?

Jack   When my father bought Shelford in 1937 there were nine people including the foreman working there, but he was a working farmer himself and reduced it to three – four when I left school - and when he took over Folly there were three more so there were seven altogether and for a number of years. And then, as things got more mechanised, we had a ploughman on each farm and a tractor driver on each farm and a fruitman.

Heather   I calculate that you were twelve years old when you went to Shelford.

Jack   Thirteen, actually

Heather   So you were still a schoolboy. Where did you go to school?

Jack   I was a day scholar at a boarding school at Herne Bay. I was a dayboy – I used to cycle in summer and cycle down to Brockman's garage in Sturry and leave my cycle there and catch a bus in winter.

Heather   Thinking about the farm – did you have any particular characters who used to work there?

Jack   Oh, yes, particularly Sandy – that was old Mr Love - and his son, Tom, who was our tractor driver in those days when we took over the farm. We only had one tractor - all the rest of the work was done with horses. Old Mr Love was an interesting character in that he chewed baccy and he used to spit with great accuracy – especially when my father suggested he did something that he didn't want to do. Mr Gammon – Bill Gammon – used to work for us and his children Cecil and Freda used to walk from Shelford along the railway line to school at Sturry. You know all about Jack Collard, of course?

Heather   I would like you to tell me about him.

Jack   Well, Jack was a thatcher. He was our thatcher and I presume he would have been a trusser as well. My great-grandfather started as a hay trusser when hay was carried loose, before balers came in. They would truss the hay out, cutting it with a knife into bale shapes and tie it so I imagine Jack might have been a trusser, too.   We still have two corn dollies hanging in my house that he made for my wife.

Heather   Tell me about the men's wages.

Jack   I remember very clearly someone getting a job as a plate-layer on the railway which meant that he was getting £3's a week instead of the 48/- shillings a week that a farm worker got. But of course it was all so relative, wasn't it?   You see, agricultural land then was worth £20 an acre and now (2001) it's worth £3000 [it is still worth £3000 an acre in 2006] so it's very difficult to make proper comparisons.   Quite a lot of farm-workers' families relied on summer overtime to buy the children's winter clothing.   That was standard practice. They'd do harvest work – before you had wheat sprays there was an awful lot of handwork to do in cereals as well as in vegetables, spudding thistles and pulling charlock.

Heather   Did your family have a car?

Jack   Yes. I can just remember the first one my father had which was a bull-nosed Morris Tourer. The first time my father took it out he was terribly proud because until then he had had a motor-bike and sidecar but it was raining and the roof leaked like nobody's business.

Heather   What about a telephone?

Jack   Yes, we had a telephone from the word go although we had a great problem with it for years and years. Even after I was married in 1956 we were still having the same problem and that was that telephone wires went down our road, across the marshes and across the river to the Sturry Road where they linked with the main line. The perishing swans would keep knocking them down and we go to use the telephone and it would be unusable and nine tenths of the time it was that the swans had broken the wires. . . .

Les Moran and the potato harvesters at Vale Farm, Broak Oak

A Child of the Fifties

By Heather Stennett

The Broad Oak of my childhood was different in many ways to present day Broad Oak. The village has grown, the first row of bungalows being built in 1959 by T.G.Kelk, Ltd., on land previously owned by Tom and Aggie Pout of the Oast House. Gradually more of the land adjoining the through road in Sweechgate and its junction with Shalloak Road has been developed. Some older houses were demolished to make way for the new development. As a child in the Fifties the road was part of our playground. Few cars were owned by villagers and the general volume of traffic going to Canterbury only started to swell in the late 1960's when Broad Oak was 'discovered' as a route to Canterbury, avoiding the congestion at Sturry.

Skipping ropes, usually lengths of old washing lines, would be strung from side to side of the road. Skipping games would involve a wide age range of the girls singing:

'I call in my very best friend, my very best friend, my very best friend. I call in my very best friend while I go out to play.'

The person skipping would sing out the chorus and swap places with the friend they had named. Often long bouts of being the one on the end holding the rope were necessary before the older girls would let me take part - unless the rope belonged to me and then of course I was able to take part in all the games!

Next to the Oast house there was a brick wall, now demolished, near the road. This was a favourite place for playing various games of ball. Careful, cautious play was called for. If the ball went over the top of the wall it was deemed lost forever. Tom and Aggie Pout had long tired of requests of 'Please can I have my ball back'. When we became their neighbours and friends and Tom Pout presented me with a bucket of 'lost balls' to play with, I felt rich beyond all measure! Go-karts of the push along sort were often going up and down the road. Raymond and Pam Beecham had a very 'posh' car made on a pram base by their father, Ted. It was the envy of many; it even had a roof.

Nowadays there is a lot of encouragement for people to organise walking buses to and from school. As a child I was lucky as my father in his job as travelling salesman for Baldwins of Canterbury had a car, so I was often taken to school in the mornings if he was going to work at that time. Dad's car could have easily competed with the Guinness Book of Records for the number of children who could be crammed into an old Ford for the journey down the hill to Sturry. If a lift was not possible then I would wait at the end of the drive until the crocodile of children passed by and I would join on. It was up to the older ones to keep an eye on the younger ones. Not an adult in sight! What a change from today.

When I was young it was expected that children would go out to play. As long as you were not late back for dinner or tea, tore your clothes or came back too muddy, the day was your own. No one had watches so we judged time by the movement of farm vehicles and the hunger pangs that told our bodies that it must be mealtimes. The children's "magnet" in summertime was the Brook, fishing for minnows, jumping the stream under the bridge, racing leaves and twigs, building dams and watercourses. We rarely used nets to catch the fish. We would lie or crouch with a keen eye and cupped hands to catch them. Fish were sometimes transported home in jam jars or the 'deluxe' container, an old Oxo tin.

It is funny how it seemed possible to stay dry, but somehow that last leap of the day often ended in the wet socks or wellies full of water. We would all squelch our way back up the hill to our houses. Mum would tell me not to go to the brook anymore but I'm afraid the attraction was far too strong. I remember one time, muddy wet white socks and shoes. I managed to get home and slip inside without Mum seeing me. Safe I thought. I took off my socks and began to wash the evidence away in the large white sink. I never for one moment thought Mum would ever know that I had been to the brook. I was very surprised when she found me busily cleaning my socks and knew just what I had been up to, holding up my, not very clean, socks as evidence.

I remember a familiar sight as a young child standing on the bridge and watching an old lady go down to the brook. She stood on a concrete block and dipped an enamel jug into the stream and started to transfer the water into a large bucket. The older boys called out 'Hello Ginny, Old Ginny Pritchard' and they started to dance about in the stream a little way upstream above her. As the water muddied Ginny gave up her quest for water, muttered a few words and made her way back up the hill to her house.

When I was a child there wasn't the fear of strangers or worries that we have now for the safety of our children. I don't mean that there weren't 'odd sorts' then, or people to be wary of, but in a village where everyone knew one another and adults who knew our parents were known as auntie Ethel or uncle Howard, it gave the feeling of security. They kept an eye on us and we knew where we could go if or when we needed help. It wasn't until I was about eight or nine that I remember my parents telling me over and over again never to take sweets from a stranger or take a ride in a stranger's car. It was too early for the Moors murders but since my friends were similarly advised there must have been a tragic event which had an impact on families and the sense of freedom that we had previously experienced. As children we all used to go to the same school, see one another playing and know one another.

Within the large group of friends there were special friends, whose houses you were invited inside to play on wet days. We were always made very welcome by Mr & Mrs Robert Jackson of Cedar cottage. We were of a similar age to their daughters Charlotte and Jane. We would rehearse plays and I remember putting on a performance, to which our parents were invited, in their house. Children also got to know one another through Sunday school and village parties. Sunday school was from 10:30 – 11:30 I used to walk to chapel with Mrs Pout, she played the organ and piano. The services comprised of rousing choruses, a bible game where we were told to draw swords. We held the bible in one hand above us. We were then given a chapter and a verse and we had to search the text. The first one to find the text would go to the front and wait until all the different texts had been found. We then read our piece to the congregation.

We were also all given a blank book at the start of the year and each week we attended we were given a large stamp, with an illustration of a bible story or text to stick in the book. The chapel Christmas party and the annual outing to Folkestone were also highlights of the chapel year. To some of the children the village outing to Folkestone was their only experience of the sea side. Incredible when you think that we are only five and a half miles from the sea at Herne Bay. The Sunday school was very popular, and children from the 'estate' were ferried up to Broad Oak in Mr Hill's van. Sometimes he had to make several trips on a Sunday to bring up all the children wanting to attend. The collection purse – a blue velvet one – was passed around while we sang:

Hear the pennies dropping. Listen while they fall

Everyone for Jesus, he shall have them all

Dropping, dropping, dropping, dropping, hear the pennies fall

Everyone for Jesus he shall have them all.

Sometimes not all of the pennies we had been given were placed in the collection, afterwards we would guiltily go to the corner shop to buy our penny chews and blackjacks. Our guilt was partly consoled by the second verse of the chorus hymn

If we have no money, we can give our love,

He'll accept our offering smiling from above.

There were at one time 3 shops in the village. Mrs Fullagar's – fancy goods, toys, sweets, cigarettes. Ron and Nora Birch Groceries and Albert and Arthur at the Post Office. I remember the first time I was sent to the post office on an errand. I was only about 5 or 6, my grandmother had asked me to buy something for her. I stubbornly refused to let her write it down. All the way along the road I repeated her order over and over again, all went well until I got inside the shop. When Arthur asked me what I wanted my mind went blank and I burst into tears. I ran back to my Nan's and I was dispatched again, this time with a note. The inside of the stores held a certain magic, jars of sweets, sides of bacon waiting to be sliced on the whirling red slicing machine, brass scales and packets of Brooke Bond tea containing picture cards to collect. The shop had a freezer with ice cream and lollies in it. The ice cream man used to come regularly to the village - as they still do – but if we wanted ice cream for pudding in the summer, (in the days before freezers were common) then at the end of the first course I would run or bike to the shop. A brick of Lyons or Walls vanilla was brought, sometimes Neapolitan, wrapped in layers of newspaper to insulate it and the dessert was rushed home. Of course mealtimes had to coincide with the time of the shops reopening after their lunch hour!

From Arthur and Albert's or Ron and Nora's shop we would buy a single slice of luncheon meat or corned beef, a packet of crisps and a bottle of red or white Bing. This made the perfect picnic for the various camps we made in the summer. The money

for such ventures was usually provided for by our finding deposit bottles which we took to the shop or pub for a refund. A penny here, and a penny there soon mounted up. The more enterprising amongst us were known on occasions to pick flowers from our parents gardens and hedgerows and 'sell' small bunches of flowers to our 'aunties' and other grown ups. The local shops did not sell newspapers or comics. To get these the villagers had to turn to Mrs Morris's Newsagents in Sturry. My Nan collected her pension from the post office in Sturry and I would often walk to Sturry with her. As a treat she sometimes brought me a Beano, Dandy or Topper comic. The comics were read over and over again before being swapped with friends.

When we look back the summer days seem warmer and longer. It's easy to remember only the good bits. The wet days or the winter days when the brook was in flood at times, seemed endless. The first sprig of Pussy Willow or Catkins for the nature table at school was a sign of summer coming again. Games, like the seasons, came and went. No-one actually said anything but there was a seamless transition from marbles to flick cards to jacks to skipping and around we would go again. The first real craze to hit us was the Hoola Hoop and this disrupted the 'normal' pattern for a while. Television did play a part in our lives but children's programmes were limited - Lunchtime television for young children. Monday Picture Book, Tuesday Andy Pandy, Wednesday Bill and Ben, Thursday Rag Tag and Bobtail and Friday The Wooden Tops. The afternoon shows for older children included The Lone Ranger, Crackerjack and Lassie. If you were lucky enough to have a new television that could pick up ITV then Popeye, Robin Hood and William Tell took hold of our imagination. The television was a focus to family life. Sunday evening was bath-time and Sunday Night at the London Palladium.

I remember clearly May 6th 1960, Princess Margaret's Wedding day. We all sat around the television dressed in our best clothes to watch the ceremony, talking in hushed voices. My parents did allow me out to play once the transmission switched from Westminster Abbey to the return to Buckingham Palace and I raced to my friend Cherry [Collard]'s house where she was similarly attired, in her best clothes, for the important event! Life was different then. To me it was a magical childhood and I hope that my memories may have stirred similar thoughts about what was special in our formative years.

A Tale I've been told
By Heather Stennett

One evening in the nineteen-twenties when my father Phil Stennett and Teddy Port, the son of the farmer at Goose Farm, Mr Edward J. Port, were young lads, they learned that the women who worked on the farm had been asked to go back that night to pick mangels – or mangolds - by moonlight.

The two youngsters plotted to scare the women out in the fields by appearing as ghostly apparitions, planning to achieve this by covering themselves in white sheets and carrying lighted candles in jam jars. As dusk fell they hid in a ditch near the field and were getting ready to carry out their plan when all of a sudden they heard a horrible groaning, shrieking and rattling of chains. According to my Dad, their feet hardly touched the ground as they raced home in their old sheets.

THE GOLDEN LION BAT AND TRAP TEAM, 1922
Back row: Gil Neaves, General Keem, Jo Styles, Tom Studham. Middle Row: Fred Whittaker, Jack Baker, Bunch Keem, Bob Keem, Tom Allen, Ted Dale. Front row: Ernie Keem, Jack Keem, Macdonald Milliner, Bob Ingleton, Steve Hollands, Frank Cackett, Fred Atkins.

BROAD OAK FOOTBALL CLUB

present

A CHARITY MATCH

between

BROAD OAK

v.

T.V. WRESTLERS

at

BROAD OAK'S GROUND

SUNDAY, 1st DECEMBER, 1968

Kick-off 2.45 p.m.

in aid of PARKVIEW PLAYING FIELD, STURRY

Lucky Programme No 2063

REFRESHMENTS
CAR PARK FREE

———

Admission by
SOUVENIR PROGRAMME
Price - 2/6

BROAD OAK TEAM

(Colours : ALL RED)

C. CLACKSON

M. SMITH   K. CLARK

T. WHITTAKER   J. ROY   J. JONES

A. ROY   G. LEGGE   T. JONES   J. SMITH   D. REDPATH

Reserves : D. CHAPMAN, F. COOK, J. TURNER

Substitute : M. GILES

Referee : JOHNNY (Head Butt) KWANGO

Linesmen : D. MATHEWS, K.C.R.A., R. CLIFTON, K.C.R.A.

Commentator : JOHN HARRIS

INTRODUCING THE HOME TEAM . . .

Broad Oak are one of the top teams of the Canterbury and District League. Formed in 1907, it has outlasted two World Wars, going from strength to strength and to-day have four football teams, ranging from Juniors to Five-a-Side. This latest venture of the Club is to encourage the local youth to participate in acquiring a playing field of their own whilst the Local Authority have on their programme a blue print for this acquisition, Broad Oak feel that every support should be given to this just cause and as such have undertaken to contribute as much as they possibly can.

To this worthwhile cause we wish the Wrestlers success in their quests to raise funds for Charity and look forward to an enjoyable afternoon.

The Remembrance of Times Past

From Link-Up – the Parish Magazine for Sturry, Broad Oak, Fordwich Westebere and Hersden, August, 1996

The annual Children's and Old Folks parties were a great feature of village life in the years that followed the last war. They were carefully timed to come after the excitements of Christmas had died down, and were organised by the Broad Oak Hut Committee under the chairmanship of Albert Hadlow, with Bob Collingwood as Honorary Secretary. Committee members included T.Alan Champion, P.T.S.Brook, Cecil Gammon and Fred Jordan. Funds for the parties were raised strictly within Broad Oak itself: by donations, a Christmas Whist Drive, and sometimes by carol singing from a lorry (complete with piano!) .

The event has been remembered with great nostalgia for nearly sixty years by those who were children then as a very real treat and a highlight of the year. All children under 14 were invited – one of them still recalls the tremendous excitement of having a present from Father Christmas with her own name on it; another the 'going home' parcel of oranges and sweets; for yet another it was the jellies, ice cream and cake in those days of austerity which have left a lasting impression.

Albert Hadlow was Father Christmas and Bob Collingwood the Master of Ceremonies – which included such games as Musical Chairs. Entertainment for the Old Folks included the de Broy Summers Band and a rendition by Pearl Castle of "I'll Take You Home, Kathleen", while Albert Hadlow sang his own favourite – "Home on the Range". Their fare included Winklewine – a type of Port wine (but said not to be so strong).

The considerable logistics of catering for up to sixty children and Old Folks were in the hands of a team that included Mrs Pearl Castle, Mrs Dot Gammon, Mrs Marjorie Maidment, Mrs Rose (Topsy) Moran, Mrs Sheila Moran, Mrs Molly Rose, Mrs Beatrice Baldock, Mrs Annie Collingwood, Miss Kit Collingwood, Mrs Dolly Fallon, Mrs Ella Gammon, Mrs Agnes Gisby, and Mrs Kath Jordan. They provided the cutlery and china from their own homes, which was where they also did all the preparation and cooking – and this for something like fifteen years. On one celebrated occasion some of the food came to grief in a car en route along Sweechgate, but nobody went without. . . .

The Revd T.Gerald Williams, Vicar of Sturry,1949-1956, Albert Hadlow of Sweechgate Stores and Edward J.Port of Goose Farm, Broad Oak.

Photograph by Derek Butler

Photograph by Michael L. Gisby

The Broad Oak Old Time Dance Club in the Milner Court Barn in the late nineteen-fifties.

From back left: Nigel Fallon, Horace Sladden, Alan Roy, Bob Murphy, Peggy Cowley, George Thundow, Margaret Thundow, Sheila Gammon, Les Baldock, Ellen Beecham, Hannie Duhoux (Monica Headley's Dutch friend), Brenda Tedham, Sheila Moran, Doris Wellard, Winifred Sladden, Annie Collingwood, Edith Tedham, Jane Murphy and Shirley Edwards.

Photograph by courtesy of Kentish Gazette

Annual Old Folks Christmas Party

Among those present were Albert Hadlow, Fred Whittaker, Mrs Jessie Townsend, Mrs Molly Rose, Mrs Ethel Brook, Ellen Beecham, Arthur and Winifred Webb, Mrs Jane Tomlin, the Revd. T.G.Williams, Mrs Lily Birch, Dick and Jenny Pritchard, Mrs Whiting, Mrs Harriet Ward, Kit Collingwood, Beatrice Baldock, Mrs Edith Tedham, Ella and Sheila Gammon, Miss Goodburn, Mrs Scott, Mr and Mrs Harry Murphy, Mr and Mrs Fred Jordan, Mr and Mrs E.O.Port, Bob Collingwood, Mr and Mrs Impett, Tom Wells, Joe Styles, Mrs Williams, Mrs Lamprell, Mrs Granville, Peggy Chaplin.

Photograph by courtesy of David Matthews

Vale Farm, circa 1909, with Mary Jane, Vera and Ella Matthews on lawn.

Photograph by kind permission of The Kentish Gazette

Members of the Broad Oak Women's Institute, Summer 1970.

Those present include Mary Allsworth, Mary Baker, Carol Gisby, Sue Brown, Brenda Child, Dorothy Delderfield, Winifred Doughty, Mabel Dunn, Susan Edwards, Molly Edwards, Ruby Fenner, Ella Gammon, Rhoda Gower, Martha Grier, Margaret Harris, Alexandra Hills, Jose Metcalfe, Jaqueline Moran, Gwyneth Morton, Dorothy Phillips, Iris Redden, Mollie Rose, Joan Speed, Jessie Townsend, Sheila Vinton, Brenda Watts, Winifred Wells, Christina Wilkinson, Josephine Wilkinson, Joy Wilson and Joan Wood.

Down in the Valley

By Graham Kenmir

The secluded stretch of the Sarre Penn valley which lies to the north of Broad Oak village has long played its part in the life of the village. For some it has been the place where they lived and worked, for others it has been a haven of unspoiled charm and for generations of children the Sarre Penn brook has proved an irresistible magnet for watery fun. However now Broad Oak Valley is a name recognised far and wide beyond the immediate area as the potential site for a new surface water reservoir. As early as 1946 mention was made in a hydrological survey of Kent of the valley as a suitable site for a reservoir as a potential source of water supply for North East Kent. Since then the valley has been described as either the most suitable or perhaps the only site for such a reservoir in Kent. By the 1970s the Southern Water Authority and the Mid Kent Water Company were arguing for the construction of a reservoir. It was envisaged that new water supplies would be needed by 1979. To meet this need construction would have to start in 1976 with the necessary permissions obtained in 1975. Fortified by the belief that these things would happen the Mid Kent company began in 1972 to negotiate to acquire the necessary land. By 1975 this first objective had been achieved. The next step of acquiring the permissions proved rather more elusive and far from being achieved in the early summer of that year, it has still not been managed thirty-one years later.

The Broad Oak Reservoir Scheme envisaged an area of 640 acres capable of holding 5400 million gallons of water. Water could be extracted from the river Stour during periods of high flow and pumped to a reservoir formed in the valley by a dam between Fox Hill and Calcott Hill to the west of the A291 Herne Bay road. The scheme would also include recreational facilities. These proposals met with considerable opposition from local groups, Parish Councils and Friends of the Earth who all argued that it would be irresponsible to flood the valley unless the need for the water was established beyond doubt. The matter was eventually submitted through a Public Enquiry to the Secretary of State for the Department of the Environment in July 1979. In November 1980 Michael Heseltine published his decision to reject the scheme, arguing that it 'over provided for the future and that with the present need to contain public expenditure, a cheaper solution should be sought on a smaller scale'. To those who did not want to suffer the loss of the valley this came as a welcome stay of execution if not as a complete reprieve. But for the Mid Kent Water it meant that rather than being the owners of a reservoir they had inadvertently become the owners of a small corner of the Garden of England.

In saying that a cheaper and smaller scheme should be sought the Secretary of State's judgement implied that a different scheme which made fewer demands on public expenditure would prove acceptable. This no doubt encouraged Mid Kent water to retain its possession of the land. It seemed likely that some day the question of a reservoir would be raised once more. Sure enough in 1989 along came the Broad Oak Water proposal. By this time the situation had

changed somewhat: the 'statutory water companies' and the water authorities had been replaced by the newly privatised water companies. Three of these companies, Mid Kent Water Company, Southern Water Services and the Folkestone and District Water Company joined forces as the sponsors of the Broad Oak Water project. A press pack was published in November of 1989 resurrecting the 640 acre 1974 scheme and giving an outline timetable for consultation and implementation. By 1990 the companies had recognised the need to base any proposal for new resources on an examination of a range options based on a comprehensive environmental assessment.

Engineering and Environmental consultants were appointed and consultations begun. In July 1991 Binnie and Partners produced an issues and options document entitled 'Water for the future of Kent.' Having given consideration to a wide range of issues, the report identified eleven combinations of options. All but one of these included the construction of a reservoir at Broad Oak. Once again a lively debate ensued as to the necessity advisability and justification of the £66 million scheme, local and national bodies raising their concerns. One of these was that the projections of future needs seemed to take little account of the possibility of reducing the demand for water. The notion that the water companies should simply provide as much water as everybody might ask for began to be replaced by a concern to limit demand and to use water wisely. These ideas have now become an accepted part of water debates but they were new ideas to many in 1990. Another major concern was whether the River Stour could withstand the extractions which would be needed to fill the proposed reservoir. There were also concerns around how far the scheme could be funded by extra charges to existing customers. How much any of these concerns weighed with the water companies is not known. This time the matter was not put to the test. In 1993 the Companies announced that they would not be putting in an immediate planning application, but that they would do so as and when required. Once again the future of the valley became uncertain.

In 2004 the reservoir scheme came back on the agenda as one of the options in the Mid Kent Water Company's consideration of Kent's New Strategic Water Resource. The current thinking is that the £100 million scheme could once again be shelved indefinitely if there is a sufficient increase in efficiency of use. Failing this, there is talk of a new planning application around 2008 with water being available by 2019. So here we are again, back to the future !

It is doubtful whether anyone would have predicted in 1975 when Mid Kent Water Company had acquired the land in the valley that it would still be being farmed thirty years later. Least of all the Water Company itself. Because work on the reservoir was expected to begin almost at once there was no need to think about what to do with the land and the houses which had been bought from a number of different owners. However once it became clear that work on the reservoir would not start for at least one year there was a need to start taking some decisions. These initial decisions which were taken as short term stop gap measures were to radically affect the valley for the subsequent three decades.

A large part of the land was bought from the Champion family at Vale farm. This included a important collection of farm buildings, with barns dating back to the 1400s and the farm house originating from 1635 with substantial 'modernisations' added in 1645. It would seem that the land had been farmed continually from early times. The range of buildings included a 'new' barn from 1750s, oasts from the 1820s and Dutch barns from the 1950s and stood as a testament to changing farming practices through the ages. Four hundred years of farming history could be detected in these buildings. This living history was soon to come to an end.

Blaxland, another mediaeval farm incorporating an early hall house, was bought by the water company from the Tharp family, along with Little Mayton. A third historic farm, Mayton ,was bought from Imhoff family. This was the site of a sixteenth century farm house which was demolished in 1953. It housed a large four kiln oast house. This is evidence of the importance of the farm as a hop-growing area owned in the first half of the nineteenth century by the Bass brewing family of Burton-on-Trent. Two of the fields in the valley are still known as Big Burtons and Bottom Burtons. Mayton Hop Farm as it was then known was bought in 1875 by the local artist Thomas Sidney Cooper who lived at Allcroft Grange which he had built at the Tyler Hill end of the valley. Hops were still being grown in this area in the 1970s and the Water Company bought some of this land from Mr Stevens as part of their reservoir purchases. The other substantial acquisition was Brambles or Bramble Bush Farm bought from Miss Mathews. This farm had been run by her father during the 1920s and the Bungalow and farm buildings were built in around 1925. It had once been part of Vale Farm. These acquisitions, along with some land near the Herne Bay Road bought from Rowbothams Nurseries, as well as one or two smaller pieces and properties completed the purchases that the Water Company needed if it was to build the reservoir. This relationship between living and working in the valley was brought to an end by the Water Company's ownership.

As far as the land was concerned it was an end to the mixed farming involving crops, cattle and pigs in favour of arable farming and initially potatoes, a very suitable crop for a short term project. Yet even this was to come under threat from an unexpected quarter. The mid 1970s saw the rise of pop festivals. What better place for a festival than a secluded valley, at once relatively removed from any substantially built up area yet very close to a major city and moreover, an area of land which was due to be flooded in the near future? Those seeking a site for a major People's Free Festival in 1976 may have thought that the valley would be a non-contentious choice. The Water Company, local opinion and concern for the potatoes meant that it turned out otherwise. The authorities got wind of what was afoot, the police arrived and the festival didn't. The potatoes were saved.

As the years rolled on and no reservoir came Vincent Brealy and then his son Andrew farmed in the Valley, eventually acquiring the use of Mayton farm and a part of the old hop garden. The appearance of the valley was much enlivened for a number of years in the 1990s when Andrew Brealy introduced the growing of daffodils on a commercial scale for the sale of the bulbs. Like Wordsworth, some people may prefer their daffodils 'beside the lake, beneath the trees, fluttering and dancing in the breeze' but there is no doubt that the synchronised swaying of the serried yellow ranks was its own kind of spectacle. To add to the enjoyment, Andrew was always ready to invite individuals and groups to visit the fields when he would be on hand to provide an interesting and informative commentary on the whole operation.

Unfortunately this diversion was not to last. In the epic struggle of man against nature or, in this case, daffs against clay, nature and clay won. To prepare the bulbs for sale it was essential to dig them up at the right point in their cycle. Unless the ground had been softened by rain, getting them out of the baked clay could be rather like extracting them from concrete. Too much rain caused other sorts of problems. Another major factor was the difficulty of recruiting enough reliable people at short notice to garner the bulbs. After contending with the perversities of the Kentish weather for a number of seasons the daffodil operation was continued elsewhere and the valley reverted to more traditional crops. So the valley which in 1974 was home to a number of families employing a variety of farming methods is now being run as one concern for arable farming. It may well be that even if the valley had not attracted the attention of the Water companies changes in farming practices may have resulted in much the same outcome that we see to-day. Perhaps it would have happened more gradually. It seems certain however that the prospect of the eventual flooding of the valley has been a deterrent to any new building. This has helped to sustain its quiet charm but has not necessarily worked to the advantage of the buildings that existed in 1974.

POST SCRIPT

The Mid-Kent Water Company, with its partners the Southern and Folkestone and Dover water companies, want to flood the valley of the Sarre Penn stream with a reservoir almost three kilometres long. The scheme, which would store water pumped from the nearby River Stour would cost about £100 million. Planned for completion in 2019, it was first proposed in 1946, when geologists found that, in a landscape of porous chalk, the valley is lined with clay that would suit a reservoir. But a planning inspector in 1980 vetoed it as "damaging and intolerable to local communities". It would, he said, take 70 per cent of the flow of the Stour, damaging the river's wetland nature reserves. Now the scheme is back on the agenda because Kent, the driest county in England, is desperate for water to supply the tens of thousands of new houses the Government wants to build there.

From "Stormy Waters" by Fred Pearce in "The Daily Telegraph Magazine", 23rd September, 2006. Fred Pearce's most recent book is

WHEN THE RIVERS RUN DRY: What happens when our water runs out ? (Eden Project Books)

The Lost Cottages of the Broad Oak Valley

by Paul Crampton

When an old property is demolished and the site not immediately redeveloped, it is amazing how quickly nature reclaims the area and soothes the wounds made by man's occupation. Such is the case with the nine properties lost in the Broad Oak Valley since the Second World War. The casual traveller will be unaware that a cottage ever stood on the overgrown plot as he or she passes by, but the more observant walker will notice the clues. What is that overgrown garden rose doing spilling through the long since unclipped Privet hedge? Why is there an isolated wire-free telegraph pole in that thicket?

The first demolition casualties were victims of a new Bridge-Blean Council policy concerning isolated properties with no mains water supply or alternative sanitary or reliable source. One such property was Copt Hall, standing on rising ground to the north of the Sarre Penne and about half a mile east of Calcott Hill. What appeared to be a late 18th century brick cottage was in fact built on the site of a Wealden hall house of some note. The property is thought to have stood derelict for some time when it was demolished in 1963. In February 2001, the hard-to-reach site gave little clues that a house had once stood there, but a concrete floor and the brick foundations of an outer wall was discovered beneath a thin layer of moss and matted grass.

Pulled down at the same time and for the same reason were Blaxland Bungalows. These curious dwellings could be found along the edge of a field and backing onto woodland, just north east of Blaxland Farm. The two adjoining L-shaped properties appeared to be of late 18th, early 19th century date, but were built around a central very ornate brick chimney in Elizabethan style, but certainly older than the bungalows. It is likely that the chimneystack had survived from an earlier timber-framed property and was substantial enough to be retained in the later rebuild. Last owned by the local farmers, the Tharp family, Blaxland Bungalows were effectively tied cottages, used by labourers and family members alike. For many years the left-hand bungalow was occupied by Peter Sparkes and his sister Flo. Peter worked for Lew Tharp. They were known to be very eccentric. They would walk all the way to Canterbury and back for their shopping. Flo was very reserved and would speak to no one. If she encountered any one who knew her, she would kneel to tie her shoelaces rather than have to make eye contact or speak with them. Her reaction to unexpected callers at Blaxland Bungalows was to run into the surrounding woods. Peter eventually developed Parkinson's disease. In the early 1960's, when Bridge-Blean council declared the Bungalows unfit for human habitation, the Sparkes were moved to a council flat in Sturry High Street.

Lew Tharp lived in the right-hand Blaxland Bungalow, and his son Malcolm was born there. In the 1930's, Lew moved to the newly built bungalow Greenacres. Jimmy Wilson, whose family lived at Blaxland Cottage, and then moved into the vacant Bungalow. He was a bachelor, and one day was found dead in the woods. After having been condemned, the dwellings were demolished in 1963 by Malcolm Tharp, who

by then, was the occupant of the bungalow 'Greenacres' to the south of Blaxland Farm, with his young family. Having stood derelict for many years under water board ownership, Greenacres was sold in 1985 to Herman Buchan, who has carried out extensive and impressive restoration work.

Blaxland Cottage stood just to the south of the bungalows and east of the Blaxland Farm complex. The brick-built property probably dated from around the late 17th century and had a substantial cat-slide roof at the rear. The Wilson family lived at Blaxland Cottage about one hundred years ago. Their son Dick continued to live at the cottage until the early years of the Second World War, by which time his parents had died, and he was called up. For many years, the cottage remained empty, and then fell into a state of disrepair. When Jim Tharp married, he moved across the field from Blaxland Farm to Blaxland Cottage.

Threatened with demolition for the same reason as the above properties, Blaxland Cottage was extensively modernised by Jim Tharp in the early 1960s, including the provision of mains water and a septic tank. It passed to water board ownership in the mid-1970s, when the reservoir plans were being pursued. Its remoteness made letting the cottage difficult and inevitably, dereliction and vandalism followed.

Demolition occurred in around 1985. As of February 2001, the site of Blaxland Cottage was a waterlogged bramble patch. However, beneath the scrub could be seen the septic tank and chunks of demolition material. Further scratching around in the mossy ground revealed the red-painted scullery floor and external wall foundations relating to the south (side) elevation. Former occupant Dick Wilson died in 2001, aged 92.

Having passed by the surviving house 'Brookside', Mayton Lane crosses the Sarre Penn, before climbing between steep banks and branching out to serve the surrounding farmsteads. Perched high on the ascending bank to the right, could once be found two pairs of brick built farm cottages known for many years (and on old maps) as Vale Cottages. Probably built in the early 19th century, they were the tied cottages of Vale Farm, situated in the valley a few hundred yards to the east. The lower pair numbers 1 and 2 were only a few yards from the Sarre Penn at the start of the upward slope to the right.

The upper pair of Vale Cottages (numbers 3 and 4) could once be found just over half way up the slope and perched much higher on the bank to the right. In 1925, they had passed to the ownership of Brambles Farm, recently created by George Matthews from about one third of Vale Farm.

Dick and Ginny Pritchard lived at No. 1 Vale Cottages. They were very self sufficient. Frank Macey remembered their immaculately-kept garden, and that their living room always smelled of old wine and apples. He used to see the bent figure of Dick walking up to the woods every day with his old dog. The cottage remained very old-fashioned and never had any modern facilities. When a large crack appeared in the end wall of No. 1, Frank used to tease Ginny that it had been caused by the weight of all the money in the loft!

Originally a man named Jock and his artist wife lived at No. 2 . They were followed by Jim and Hilda Williams. Jim was a miner and a huge man and Hilda was tiny. They eventually moved to Sturry, and later died there, within half an hour of each other. In the years immediately following the Second World War, a large crack appeared in the southern end wall of No. 1 and it became apparent that the cottages were gradually slipping into the stream. The pair were pulled down by Vale farm workers, including Les Moran, in the early 1950s.

In the late 1930's, No. 3 Vale Cottages was occupied by Bert Sparkes, brother of Peter and Flo Sparkes of Blaxland Bungalows. Bert worked for "Tanner" Lloyd, who lived on Calcott Hill. Bert and his wife had two daughters, Mavis and Mary and the family later moved to a council house in Sweechgate. After they left No. 3, Bob Carter moved in. He went to work for Neame's Bakery in Sturry, and shared a packet of cigarettes, bought with his first week's wages, with Frank Macey from No. 4. In 1946, Nick Raine and his wife Florence came to live at No. 3. Originally from Bishop Auckland, Mr Raine had moved to Canterbury, where his daughter Ada was born. Another daughter, Pat, planted a fig tree that can still be seen. In 1953, Vera Matthews, who then owned Nos. 3 and 4, had offered to sell the pair to Nick Raine for £400.00. He turned this offer down, much to the fury of Florence!

Bill and Ivy Macey moved into No. 4 Vale Cottages in 1928. Their son Frank was two months old at the time. The Macey family left No. 4 in 1937 to live at Chapel Cottages, Chapel Lane, Broad Oak. No. 4 was subsequently occupied for a time by a Mr Foreman.

By the late 1950s, the upper pair stood empty and were rapidly becoming derelict. Salvation came in 1961 when they were bought by the Delderfield family who had long wanted to own a cottage in the country. James Delderfield knocked the two cottages into one and set about an extensive modernisation programme. On completion, the new home was christened Brook Cottage. Sadly, the family spent only a few happy years together in their dream home before James died suddenly at the age of only 48. His widow Dodie hung on until 1972 before selling up to the water board. There then followed a series of renters, but all too quickly, the property became a squat. It was during this final period that Brook Cottage, like the lower pair of Vale Cottages, began to suffer from subsidence - a huge crack appeared in the rear elevation of the property, indicating its movement towards the lane below. Demolition occurred sometime around 1984. An expedition to the site in early 2001, revealed much evidence of the existence of Brook Cottage. From Mayton Lane, some stonework surrounding the steep drive could just be made out, as could over-grown evergreen trees and abandoned telegraph poles in the former garden above. From the rear, both concrete washing line poles still existed and further onto the site, the clearance of some mossy undergrowth revealed black and white linoleum tiles still adhering to the kitchen floor.

At the top of the slope up from the Sarre Penn, a track branches off from Mayton Lane to the right and descends towards Vale Farm. To the north of this junction stood a weather-boarded cottage of indeterminate date, called 'Little Mayton'. It faced due south and overlooked much of the valley. Although much closer to Mayton Farm and even sharing the name, this cottage was owned by Blaxland Farm. Eddie Tharp and his family lived here for many years, and when the Blaxland Farm set-up fragmented in 1962, ran it and the surrounding fields as a separate smallholding. The water board took over ownership in 1975, but the property became a student squat almost straight away. In 1976, Little Mayton became the headquarters of the so-called Broad Oak Pop Festival. A fire in the early 1980s, presumably caused by vandals, sealed the fate of Little Mayton and the remains were cleared away shortly afterwards. As at spring 2001, the former garden area still contains many cultivated trees and plants albeit much overgrown. The site of the cottage itself is occupied by a huge pile of earth, but with huge chunks of demolition material protruding.

Mayton Farm stands on a promontory between two shallow valleys created by the Sarre Penn and its subsidiary. The picture of the 16th century Mayton farmhouse is quite well known and shows the property in happier years during the 1920s. The farm was compulsorily taken over by the War Agricultural Executive Committee, and the house became

Tharp's Cottages, Shalloak Road, Broad Oak, during demolition, early 1960's.

derelict at about this time. Demolition occurred in 1953, shortly before the Imhof family took over ownership. They built the current modern farmhouse and dug out the foundations of the old demolished property to repair the rutty farm tracks.

Upon taking over the farm in the mid 1950s, the only habitable dwelling John Imhof found at Mayton Farm, was the former gamekeeper's cottage called 'Apsley Lodge'. This L-shaped brick cottage carried a date stone of 1859, putting it just before the lengthy tenure of painter T.Sidney Cooper. The Imhofs continued to occupy Apsley Lodge, and their parents the new house opposite . However, the lodge was condemned in 1970 and following the construction of a replacement bungalow opposite (into which the grandparents moved), Apsley Lodge was pulled down by the Imhof family, helped by the children who were paid one old penny for every roof slate they managed to retrieve whole. The combined name and date stone from the old property was placed in the garden of the new bungalow, but being of plaster construction, soon weathered away to nothing. The new bungalow continued to be referred to as 'Apsley' on modern maps, but this a cartographical error and it never received that name. Today, the site of Apsley Lodge is an impenetrable thicket and no doubt, haven for wild life.

There is one more property whilst although still standing, is lost in almost every other sense. Brambles Farm was created in 1925 by George Matthews, who sold two thirds of his Vale Farm and re-established a new farmstead on what was left. A new farmhouse, really a bungalow, was built high up on the northern slopes of the Broad Oak Valley, right on the edge of Cole Wood. The property was boarded up and an aluminium roof covering was fitted in an attempt to halt its decline after the Water Board took over. Sadly, however, the effects of both the elements and vandals have caused Brambles to decline still further. -Today, the plants, trees and shrubs of Vera Matthews's once well-tended garden, have grown into a natural shield that within a few years, will completely obscure the property from view.

Copt Hall, Calcott, photographed in 1953, former home of the Franklyn family, and latterly occupied by James Spratt after service in the Buffs in 1ˢᵗ World War. He spent the rest of his life as a shepherd for the Champion family.

Photograph by Kinn McIntosh

Architectural notes on the missing houses of Broad Oak

By Margaret J. Sparks

Tarpot Cottage: This looks early nineteenth century, like Little Mayton, but it might be earlier (it has a tiled roof), with weatherboarding for cladding.

Mayton Farm: Possibly 1550's Timber-framed with jettied upper storey which is tile-hung. Good seventeenth century chimney; eighteenth century sash windows upstairs. Two nineteenth century bay windows below.

(This is the photograph Roger Higham used for his drawing on page 29 of STURRY –THE CHANGING SCENE.)

Copt Hall: This appears to be a seventeenth century brick cottage with tiled roof and chimneys at each end.

Calcott Hall: A late eighteenth century brick house – three bays with dormers at the front with a higher extension at the

Eddie Tharp outside Little Mayton

Photograph by courtesy of Margaret James

Vale Farm Barn: This might be medieval but in any case seventeenth century – Kenneth Gravett says "early seventeenth century" in STURRY-THE CHANGING SCENE p 29

Mayton Cottages: These were built by the artist T.S.Cooper in 1906

Tharp's forge in Shalloak Road.

Photograph by courtesy of Mrs Ellen Todd

Tharp's Cottages: This is the most interesting of the missing properties and was in Shalloak Road. It is a substantial medieval or sixteenth century hall house, timber-framed, with low end cross wing. The high end cross wing has been rebuilt in brick possibly in the late eighteenth century. The hall has an inserted floor with dormer window for the upper rooms. There is an inserted chimney at the high end. A further dwelling (with chimney) has been added to the left of the photograph. This looks like a large farm house.

Blaxland Cottage: This is a late seventeenth century brick cottage, with tiled roof and chimneys at each end. It is very like Copt Hall in construction.

Blaxland Bungalows: It is hard to tell about the chimney from the rather fuzzy photograph. The cottages look rather like nineteenth century almshouse-type cottages, in a romantic style with barge boards and leaded (quarried) windows. It seems unlikely that the chimney was removed and rebuilt, and I suspect the site would be unusual for a sixteenth house with a pretentious chimney.

Hawcroft Farm: The end towards the photograph is possibly early seventeenth century, of two bays with Victorian

Photograph by courtesy of Paul Crampton

The Tharp family at Blaxland Farm, in August 1926

porch. The taller extension is perhaps nineteenth century on the grounds of the chimney and type of dormer windows. Kenneth Gravett said the older barn at Hawcroft was seventeenth century. (STURRY – THE CHANGING SCENE, p 27)

Little Mayton: An early timber-framed cottage with weather-boarding and probably a slate roof.

Apsley Lodge: This is Sidney Cooper of nearby Alcroft Grange spreading artistic housing into the landscape. Brick and tile with bargeboards and unusual windows.

Pout's Oast: The Roundel Oast Houses came in about 1835. The 1918 photograph of the oast shown - say 1840-1850.

There are also photographs of a number of cottages mostly in Mayton Lane also demolished but not illustrated here. They show very rough, early-to-mid nineteenth century farm cottages, single storey, in brick and thatched. These were always of very poor quality and have not surivived.

Photograph by courtesy of Allan Butler

Mr and Mrs D.R.Chalmers-Hunt outside Little Orchard, Barnet's Lane.

Photograph by Malcolm Tharp

Blaxland Bungalows, since demolished.

Photograph by courtesy of Malcolm Tharp

Jim Tharp and great nieces and nephew outside Blaxland Cottage.

Footnote:

Since the publication of "Sturry – The Changing Scene" in 1972 further investigations have taken place on the still existing Mead Manor in Chapel Lane, Broad Oak, which is included in A GAZETTEER OF MEDIAEVAL HOUSES IN KENT by Sarah Pearson, P.S. Barnwell and A.T. Adams (published by the Royal Commission on Historical Monuments, 1994). The house is described in detail with cross section and ground floor plans. The results of the further investigations have been published in THE MEDIAEVAL HOUSES OF KENT – An Historical Analysis by Sarah Pearson (published by the Royal Commission on the Historic Monuments of England, 1994). The timbers have been tree-ring dated to 1465 and in the opinion of the author "if this was always a house, then not only would it have been unusually small for its date, but it would also be the earliest known two-storeyed hall heated by a smoke bay" (p.106)

Little Orchard, another interesting house that is also still extant though the light at the top of the photograph causes problems. Is the white thing in the roof a dormer or the base of a chimney? Is there a chimney at the left? It is a brick cottage in Flemish Bond with tiled roof and early nineteenth century windows. If the chimney is central, it might be a lobby-entry house of the seventeenth century: otherwise possibly eighteenth century.

The Tharps of Blaxland Farm

By P D and M A Crampton

When Blaxland Farm was sold to the Water Board in 1975 and the remaining members of the Tharp family moved away from the Broad Oak valley, thus ended an association with the area that had lasted for several centuries. There had been Tharps at Blaxland Farm since the 1880's, but it is mainly the last fifty years of their tenure that will be looked at here.

John Underdown Tharp, known as "Chipper", had inherited the farm from his father, James Underdown Tharp. In 1893 he married Frances (Fanny) Tuthill, and they had nine children: Wallace, Minnie, Edwin, Lillian, John (Jack), Lewis (Lew), Kathleen, Sidney (Jim) and Margery.

When Lew Tharp married Isabel (Janet) File in 1931 they moved into one of the two Blaxland Bungalows, which stood just across the fields from the farm. Their son Malcolm was born there, and they later had two daughters: Sylvia and Jennifer. In 1936, Lew had a new two-bedroomed bungalow built for his family in the fields below his parents' farm, at a cost of £650.00. He called it "Greenacres". Jim Tharp subsequently married Janet File's sister Dorothy, and moved to the nearby Blaxland Cottage.

Edwin Tharp went to China as a missionary, returning in 1926. He married his wife Mabel two years later, and they moved to "Little Mayton", in Mayton Lane. Their only child Margaret was born there in 1932. Jack Tharp worked as a representative for the feed firm, Bibby's. He also married and had a son, as did Wallace. Minnie Tharp never married, and lived at Blaxland Farm for most of her life.

John Underdown Tharp died in 1946 leaving a will that named only four of his nine children as beneficiaries: Edwin, Minnie, Lew and Jim. The four beneficiaries formed a partnership and continued to farm at Blaxland together. Edwin remained at "Little Mayton", but ran the farm's dairy operations. He had his own milk round, delivering bottles on which was printed "J.U Tharp & Sons". He used his own Ford van for this enterprise, which ended in 1948 after which milk from Blaxland was delivered in bulk to Abbott's Dairies.

For children, Blaxland Farm must have been a fascinating place to spend their formative years. One can only imagine the idyllic summer playground provided by the rambling farmhouse, its outbuildings and the surrounding lands and woods. Conversely, its remoteness and lack of facilities must have made hard winter days seem very long and gruelling. In the snow and ice, car journeys across the valley must have been very precarious for the Tharps, who had to drive Lew's daughter Sylvia to the Simon Langton Girls' School in Canterbury each day, stopping en route at number 3 Mayton Lane to collect her schoolmate, Norma Raine.

Although Malcolm Tharp never lived in the farmhouse itself, he retains many fond memories of it. He recalled that the room immediately above the parlour was known as the "Owl" room, so named because its ceiling was bowed down due to the many years worth of owls' nests that had been built above it. Eventually the ceiling collapsed under the

weight of accumulated nest matter and droppings. An entire trailer-load of debris was carted away, as a result. With the ceiling gone, the "Owl" room was now open to the roof, which was held together by branches.

There was an external staircase at the back of the house leading to another upstairs room that was the men's dormitory . There were two other bedrooms and also one very small room that once was a gentleman's dressing room. Inside this tiny space, just beyond the door, was a small ledge for his wig-stand. All of these upstairs rooms led into one another.

On the ground floor there was a large kitchen directly below the dormitory, and a parlour beneath the "Owl" room. Next to the parlour was a large room with a stone floor. The dairy was across the hallway from the parlour. There also used to be a separate bake house whose chimney became home to a nest of bees, but this was demolished in the 1950's.

Outside, there were two thatched buildings: a stable, next to the bake house, and beyond that a barn, standing opposite the house. Leading off the barn was a structure known as the roundel, projecting out into the farm road. Peter Firmin and Oliver Postgate used the roundel in the filming of their children's TV series "Pogle's Wood", in which it featured as the "old cottage".

Standing separate from the other farm buildings were a cowshed, with capacity for a herd of twelve, and a tiled granary said to have been constructed from old ships' timbers, which stood on staddle stones. Sadly, in the 1987 hurricane, both the granary and the thatched barn were destroyed.

When Malcolm Tharp married in 1959, he and his new wife Pat moved into a caravan in the grounds of "Greenacres". In 1962, his father Lew declared his intention to go out on his own as a farmer. As a result, the partnership was dissolved and the four siblings that had formed it prepared to go their separate ways. Minnie left Blaxland Farm, where she had lived all her life, and moved to Egerton. She let her share of the farm to Lew, who moved into the farmhouse in 1963, leaving "Greenacres" free for Malcolm and his family.

It was around this time that the council condemned several properties in the area as being unfit for habitation, including Blaxland bungalows, and which were subsequently demolished. The same fate nearly befell Blaxland farmhouse, but Lew soon set about a programme of renovation and modernisation at the old house, which included the conversion of the former dormitory into a bathroom. Jim Tharp, who was still living at Blaxland Cottage, carried out similar improvements to his property, while Edwin continued to reside at "Little Mayton", from where he farmed his now segregated thirty acres of surrounding land.

When Minnie Tharp returned to the area from Egerton, she initially went to live with her sister Margery for a while, before moving into a retirement home in Whitstable. Kathleen Tharp died aged 74, and in 1971, Lew Tharp died, aged 68.

When the reservoir plans were first put forward in the early 1970's, it was proposed that a new road would be laid through the woods to Blaxland Farm, which was to become a clubhouse for the planned recreation facilities. By 1975, the Tharps had sold the farm to the Water Board, along with all their other property in the Broad Oak Valley. The buildings were boarded up and the land rented out to other farmers on a yearly licence.

Malcolm Tharp subsequently moved both his family and his Uncle Jim to Dorset. Jim Tharp died as recently as October 2002, aged 95. His sister-in-law Janet Tharp survived him for a further two years; she died in January 2004, just six months short of her 100th birthday. The Tharps' departure for new beginnings did not just mark the end of an era in their own history; it also brought to a close another long chapter in the history of Blaxland farmhouse which, for the first time in its 500 years, now ceased to be at the heart of a working farm.

Sturry's Fire Brigade

by Derek R.Butler

It was some time in 1910 that the Sturry Fire Brigade was called to Blaxland Farm in Mayton Lane to attend a blaze in the farm buildings there and it was a tribute to the speed at which they turned out that they not only arrived there before the fire caught hold but in time to preserve the strings of paper which were criss-crossing the building at ceiling level in an attempt to help the fire on its way. Later that year a man called Thornby, whose father was an employee of the Tharps, was acquitted at Maidstone Sessions of setting the fire.

In the nineteenth century fire-fighting was mainly in the hands of Insurance Company brigades' volunteers, supplemented, as in the case of Canterbury, by policemen who doubled as fire-fighters. In 1901 the Canterbury Police Fire Brigade operated from the old police station in Pound Lane adjacent to the Westgate Towers and had at its disposal a fire escape ladder together with hose and stand pipes. The ladder can be seen in old photographs of the Towers. A letter of complaint to the Editor of "Fire and Water" in 1895 referred to the ladder: "There is an antiquated escape ladder on wheels which has stood at the police station exposed to all weathers for some years, and if used would more likely increase the danger to life than assist in saving it".

Thankfully, the local area here was covered by the County Fire Office Brigade under Captain W.G.Pidduck of Oaklands, Staines Hill, Sturry, the Phoenix Insurance Company and the Canterbury branch of the Kent Fire Office. The latter brigade had been formed in 1821 and continued until it was disbanded in 1922 when its parent company merged with the Royal Insurance Company. This Brigade worked from the old Archbishop's Palace (now part of the King's School) and had a steam engine, manual pump, 2 hose reels and 1500 feet of hose.

Leonard T Ashenden, (older residents like myself might well remember him) joined the brigade in 1891 and was promoted to Lieutenant in 1900. He was promoted Captain in 1903 and remained in this position until 1922. A qualified Surveyor, L.T. Ashenden became involved in estate management and moved to Sweech Farm in Broad Oak in 1902 before settling for the rest of his long life at Whatmer House adjoining Whatmer Hall Farm in the Island Road at Sturry. Captain Ashenden's Brigade consisted of some ten men, all volunteers, and they held regular drills in fields off the Island Road at Sturry, using the old spring in the garden of The Hillock there to top up their water supplies. This

Kent Fire Office Brigade with Lieutenant L.T.Ashenden on the railway level Crossing at Sturry.

Photography by courtesy of Derek Butler

Brigade attended many fires in the district, their last duty involving a fire in the cow sheds at Whatmer Hall Farm!

In 1913 following a number of fires at Sturry Primary School, the Headmaster, Thomas Pope, persuaded the Parish Council to purchase some fire fighting equipment, viz: 400 feet of hose, a standpipe and branches, together with a cart which was housed at the Rose Inn in Sturry High Street. Leonard Ashenden was appointed Chief Officer and was assisted by Arthur Bournes, Bill Goldfinch, Walter Jarvis and Ernest Taylor of Dengrove, all of whom received basic training. When fires occurred they were contacted by messenger! The Brigade was properly organised in 1924 and became a member of the National Fire Brigades' Association. A year later following fund-raising efforts in the village, a second hand Shand Mason steam pump (dating from 1909) was purchased from the town of Bedford. A second hand Hotchkiss taxi was then converted into a tender by Bligh Bros of Canterbury to tow the steam pump - which took six minutes to get steam up.

The funeral of Fireman Ben Baker with the Revd Samuel Risdon Brown (Vicar of Sturry, 1938-1949) and Chas W Lyons approaching St Nicholas Church, Sturry.

Photograph by courtesy of Derek Butler

At this time Percy Brooker was appointed First Officer with Edward J.Port, Snr., of Goose Farm, Broad Oak, as his deputy. Charlie Burton, licensee of the Rose Inn at Sturry, became the First Engineer and he was responsible for alerting the volunteer firemen by firing a maroon over the cricket field. They also had little plaques, long-gone, by their front doors advising the public that a fireman lived there.

The brigade attended some major fires in the late 1920's and 1930's including those at Deanery Farm, Chartham, Fordwich House in 1928, the Fordwich Arms in 1930, Canterbury tannery in 1931, Old Tree Farm at Hoath and Denne's Mill in Canterbury in 1933 and Kent College in 1938. They were also involved in pumping out local properties during the floods of December, 1927, when Sturry Church was under water.

At this time other members of the brigade included Frank Cackett, Harry Seath, Bob Collingwood (later to become Sub-Officer) , Bob Lucas, Ernest Banks, George Bubb, George Lamb, Ernie Brenchley, Sid Amos, Ted Farrier, Teddy Port, Arthur Bournes (Secretary), Percy Philpott, Reg Maile, Len Dale and Ben Baker. The latter died in the late 1930's and his coffin was borne to St Nicholas Church on the fire tender driven by George Bubb, Ben's fellow firemen forming a guard of honour

The Brigade made a name for itself by winning the South-Eastern District Competition for the Westbrook Shield in the years 1929 to 1932 and again in 1934 as well as other trophies. It became part of the National Fire Service when this was formed in August 1941 and the appliances were garaged behind "Fernleigh" in Fordwich Road, from where the siren was operated. Members played a major part in the rescue work following the blitz on Sturry High Street on the evening of 18th November, 1941 - George Bubb is particularly remembered for his efforts in attempting to rescue the occupants of the Red Lion.

The Brigade itself suffered a severe blow on the night of 6th June 1942 (German aircraft were still attacking Canterbury after the main raid of 1st June 1942) when volunteer fireman, 31 year-old William E. Ward of Sweechgate Cottages, was killed when the fire engine overturned in a bomb crater. The crew were on their way to a fire at Littlebourne, travelling without lights, when the tragedy occurred. The Sturry firemen mounted a guard of honour at his funeral and the coffin was draped in the Union Jack. The Vicar, the Revd. Samuel Risdon-Brown, said that "the fire services were part of the fighting forces of the Empire and one of them had laid down his life in their great cause. His sacrifice would not be in vain".

William is among those commemorated on the Second World War memorial in Sturry Church.

In April 1948 the new Kent Fire Brigade took over all the fire stations in the county, the year in which stalwarts Arthur Bournes and Edward J.Port, Snr., retired from the service both having been awarded the Fire Brigade's Silver Medal. It is interesting to note that Bob Collingwood gave details in the Sturry Parish magazine of the 43 call-outs that were answered during a four-month period in the summer of 1949. In 1961 the new fire station was built in Chafy Crescent to house the new Commer fire tender with many of the pre-war volunteers still on "active service".

Local people can be proud of the part played by the volunteer firemen of Sturry who gave up much of their leisure-time to protect our citizens both in Peace and War and for those "retained" fire-fighters who still protect our village community.

Sources:
Klopper, Harry , TO FIRE COMMITTED (The Whitefriars Press, 1984)
Bygone Kent Vol 1, No 7 (1980) David Ashenden "An Old Fire Brigade".
STURRY, THE CHANGING SCENE. ed K.H.McIntosh (1972):
Arthur Mackenzie "Sturry and District Fire Brigade".

THE MATTHEWS OF BRAMBLES FARM

By Mary Anne Crampton

In the mid-1970's my mother and I made the acquaintance of an elderly lady neighbour who had come to live in a beautiful, newly-built brick bungalow that looked across the fields towards our own, rather shabby, 1920's roughcast champagne-plot variety. Her name was Vera Matthews, and although we were to pay her several visits in the course of the next twenty years, we were never to get to know her as well as we would have liked to do,

She would not, for example, ever tell us her age or even the date of her birthday, although she never failed to remember our own, commemorating them by sending us cards that not only showed exquisite taste, but a mutual love of flowers and wildlife. It was on one of our visits that she talked about the house where she had been born, a house called Vale Farm, and how at the present time it stood empty and derelict, awaiting its fate of drowning beneath the proposed Broad

Oak valley reservoir. It was at that time she handed us an old photograph of the house, in the front of which stood a woman and two small girls. I was fascinated. The woman was Vera's mother, Mary Jane, and the girls Vera and her sister Ella.

During the First World War, Vale Farm was requisitioned by the Army, which arrived in 1915 demanding billets for soldiers and stabling for their horses. The house was large enough for the Matthews family to remain in their home alongside the military and when the time came for the Army to leave they presented her father, George Matthews, with a clock, complete with commemorative plaque.

After the war George Matthews wanted to scale down his farming activities and he set up Brambles Farm on the remotest 120 acres of Vale Farm land, selling his surplus stock and farm equipment by auction on 2nd January 1925. The catalogue of Frank Amos, Auctioneer, Valuer and Surveyor, of The Parade, Canterbury, included 5 young cart horses, 4 van cab mares, 29 head of horned stock and 36 head of swine. And in November 1925, builder Ernest Slingsby of Park View, Sturry, signed the House Certificate required by Blean Rural District Council under Building Bye Law no 89 to certify that Brambles Farm was ready for habitation.

The bungalow had three bedrooms and a bathroom but no mains services – the original estimate included an "earth closet to be built near house". Water was pumped up from a spring halfway between the bungalow and its outbuildings, to be carried back in buckets. Gas and oil lamps lighted the bungalow, whose fires required a constant supply of chopped wood for heating. At Brambles George Matthews developed his interest in trees and shrubs, planting many in the surrounding gardens, and an avenue of oaks alongside the lane that led to the house. He continued farming on a very small scale, keeping just sheep and a few bullocks. There were thousands of rabbits on the Brambles land and Frank Macey recalled that his father, Bill, the only farmhand there, would regularly go into Canterbury with 12 dozen rabbits hanging on sticks. There were also many pheasants and George Matthews reputedly adept at catching them.

And what of Vera? She had developed a fine singing voice, and became a member of the Canterbury Operatic Society. By the outbreak of the Second World War in 1939 George Matthews had rented out all of his land to Jesse Brockman and Vera had joined the WAAF. She was later to say that her years in the Services were amongst the happiest she had ever known. They were also very fulfilling and by 1946, "Matty", as she became known, had achieved the rank of Flight Officer on temporary promotion.

The close proximity of the Broad Oak valley to the city of Canterbury meant that it had not escaped the Blitz unscathed. On 16th June, 1942, Mr L A Johnson presented George Matthews with an estimate for repairs for "Damage caused through Enemy Action during Raids on Canterbury". Vera's career in the WAAF was ended by the deterioration in her parents' health and on 12 June 1949 George Matthews died at the age of 87 at Brambles Farm and was buried in Sturry cemetery. Six years later – on 11 December, 1955, Mary Jane Matthews died at home at the age of 89.

Vera Matthews in her garden in front of Brambles Farm

Photograph by David Matthews

After her mother's death Vera continued to live at Brambles entirely alone, still without mains water or electricity, still lit by gas and oil lamps. She would walk all the way to Broad Oak to catch the bus to Canterbury, wearing Wellington boots as far as the top of Mayton Lane, changing there into footwear more suitable for the town and leaving her boots in the hedge.

What changed her way of life was contained in a letter dated 3rd October, 1967, when the Canterbury and District Water Company sent in reply to a letter sent to them by Vera two days earlier regarding "The Broad Oak Impounding Scheme". Although it begins by stating "The work on this scheme is at present in the very early stages, and no site surveys or details have been agreed", it concludes with a paragraph beginning with this disturbing sentence: "It would appear that there may be a problem of access to your property should this scheme proceed…" Enclosed with their letter was a plan clearly showing that Brambles would be surrounded on three sides by water, meaning that any future access could only be through the woodlands behind. This cannot have been a very reassuring prospect for a 63 year-old woman, living on her own.

In May, 1972, affected landowners were sent a circular in which terms were set out regarding "Compensation for Compulsory Purchase". By June, 1974, Vera had agreed to sell. It must have been some comfort to her to read in a letter from the solicitors that same month that "…..Clause 3 mentions that the Board will endeavour to promote a bird sanctuary or nature reserve in the yellow area on the plan".

One could be sure that Vera, who died on 18th August, 1996, at the Whitstable and Tankerton Hospital, would have done her utmost to ensure that the welfare of her feathered friends would continue to be a consideration even after she herself would no longer be there to care for them.

The Champion Family – Fifty years at Vale Farm

by PD and MA Crampton

Thomas Champion acquired Vale Farm in 1925 from George Matthews, who was moving to his newly built bungalow "Brambles". Before coming to the Broad Oak valley, Thomas and his wife Fanny - who came from a Thanet farming family - had farmed at Sarre Court. They had three children: Thomas Alan (always known as Alan), Doreen and Maud.

The old barn at Vale Farm, Summer 1974.

Photograph by courtesy of Averil Akehurst

When Alan married, he and his wife Winifred moved into Barnet's Cottage, Barnet's Lane, Broad Oak. Their daughter Averil was born in 1948, and they also had a son, Anthony, always known as Tony. (Alan's sister Maud married farmer Percy Spanton, and they moved to Barfrestone Court, near Dover.) Doreen continued to live with her parents at Vale Farm. Thomas Champion, senior, retired in 1940 and died when his granddaughter Averil was very young and the farming operation was taken over by his son. In the late 1950's, Alan Champion employed the building firm Else to construct a new house close to Vale Farm, for his widowed mother and his sister, planning that he and his family would then move into the much larger Vale Farm house. Before these moves could take place, Fanny Champion fell ill and ironically was better placed by remaining in the old house which, unlike its new neighbour, had heating. Consequently, Alan Champion and his family moved into the new house – never officially named "New" Vale Farm – much to his daughter Averil's chagrin, as she had been looking forward to living in the old house! Even after the death of Fanny Champion, this arrangement did not change, and Doreen continued to live alone and independently in the rambling farmhouse.

A young Averil Champion at the wheel of a Fordson tractor, with John and Fred Jordan behind her and Les Moran in the distance taken in 1961 or 1962

Photograph by courtesy of Averil Akehurst

It will come as no surprise to learn that Doreen was a close friend of Vera Matthews, who had spent her childhood at Vale Farm and who now lived at "Brambles". The two women had much in common. Both were spinsters who had nursed elderly parents until their deaths, and then continued to live on alone in their family homes. They were keen gardeners, loved animals and enjoyed brisk walks in the valley. They were also both fiercely independent and would neither accept, nor request, any help.

Although the Champions had most of their groceries delivered directly to the farm, Doreen preferred to make her own arrangements. Her niece Averil recalls how her Aunt would walk all the way across the valley from the farmhouse to the bus stop at the foot of Calcott Hill and Fox Hill, to go into town for her shopping. She would then return the same way, laden with her provisions. The many large rooms of Vale Farm house were dominated by pieces of furniture that were so vast they could never have fitted into any other house, yet Doreen always managed to keep the entire place scrupulously clean. One room, the drawing room, was never used at all; there was another large reception room that was always used for family get-togethers. It had a large fireplace with a wooden fire surround in which a fire was always kept burning. The farm's huge kitchen garden was also Doreen's domain, and was kept in the same immaculate condition as the house.

Photograph by courtesy of The Kentish Gazette

The barn at Vale Farm in February, 1985, prior to dismantling.

The base of the old oast at Vale Farm, February 1988

T. Alan Champion at Vale Farm, Broad Oak.

Throughout all her years as chatelaine of Vale Farm, Doreen's routine never varied. She would rise each morning at 8.00 without fail, in order to feed the chickens and to put out milk and food for the cats. At 4.00 every afternoon she would have tea with her brother. They would finish by 4.20 when Alan would then go to join the Vale Farm stockman and thatcher Fred Jordan, to assist him in feeding the pigs. Every Sunday, Doreen and her friend Vera would go for walk in the valley. For these two redoubtable ladies, a "walk" meant a brisk route march, not a gentle stroll.

The parallels in the lives of Doreen and Vera were to last until the mid-1970's when the reservoir plans led to both women leaving the homes where they had spent almost their entire lives, and had never wanted to leave. Vera moved to a new bungalow near Whitstable, and Doreen to Bridge. The huge furniture at Vale Farm was sold off, along with the rest of the contents, and Doreen bought all new. The effect of so much change late in life took its toll on Doreen. She was never really happy in her new environment, and sadly died not long after moving away from Vale Farm.

Alan Champion is remembered by all who knew him as a gentleman. Les Moran, Fred Jordan and Fred's son Bill all worked for him until 1975, when he sold the farm. Les, who had started work at Vale Farm in the 1940's, recalls that his employer was also very fond of animals, and preferred livestock farming to arable. Like his sister Doreen, he loved dogs. One in particular, named Tib, occasionally used to nip people. Even in winter, Alan Champion would always work until 6.00 pm, when he would return home, and his sheepdog would go into the doghouse – a flat roofed building at the end of the thatched granary building – as the working dogs never lived in the house.

During his tenure at Vale Farm, Alan Champion expanded the Vale Farm land to around 250 acres, and also carried out many improvements. His wife Winifred did all the bookkeeping for the farm, as well as all the cooking, and during the war, she helped out in the fields. In 1946, Les and Fred put up a new six-bay tractor shed, to house a trailer and binder, elevator and tractor. Two years later, the old barn was re-thatched by Les, his brother Joe, and Fred Jordan. A new granary was also built, which necessitated the felling of several Scots pine trees, the side walls being built up in blocks by Les's father-in-law. He also laid the concrete floor, in which he wrote the date. Les dug out a pit for the new granary, into which grain would be tipped from vehicles backed up to the door, to be bagged up by Fred. The full bags would then be moved by elevator to free up the granary for the next day's work. During the 1960's, Else Builders laid new flooring in the oast. This work also included the oast's upper storey, as the previous floor had rotted away. A new Massey combine harvester, with a bagger, was bought in 1963, and a new shed was built for it. A combine harvester that incorporated a tank was added to the farm machinery in 1967. The Champions also created two new cattle yards next to the eighteenth century barn. They kept their pigs in both the

The farmyard and oast at Vale Farm. A study of whole complex was published in Wade, Jane,(editor)TRADITIONAL KENT BUILDINGS No 6 "Vale Farm, Broad Oak, Sturry" by Lawrence Chambers and Nicholas Weedon, published by the Canterbury College of Art and Design (1988)

corrugated-iron single storey shed that faced the house, and also in the thatched range adjacent to the stable block. They always referred to the pigsties as the "Mansions".

Life at the farm wasn't all work; there was also plenty of fun to be had. For example, on Guy Fawkes' night, the

Champion children were treated to a large bonfire and fireworks in the front garden at Vale Farm. Averil remembers one occasion when her father lit a large rocket that shot straight up into a large tree, setting fire to it. Their son Tony did not follow in his parents' farming footsteps. He chose instead an academic life, becoming a professor of geography. Averil on the other hand fully embraced farming. She had her own Ford 3000 tractor, with a Whitlock trailer. Les and Fred created a tractor shed for it by knocking out the inside of the rear oast roundel. Averil also shared her father's love of animals and would take Vale Farm livestock up to the Kent County show. In 1976 she married fellow farmer Robert Akehurst and moved to her new husband's farm near Barham, where they continue to enjoy their love of the land and the company of their beloved dogs. Bob Akehurst remembers how he and Alan Champion would always share the washing up after family get-togethers. If he passed back a saucepan to him, because it still had a bit of cabbage in it, his father-in-law would reply: "Well, we're having cabbage next week, aren't we?"

As a final chapter the Water Board first approached Alan Champion in 1972, regarding the proposed reservoir and the purchase of Vale Farm. In 1974, they carried out test boring in Tarrant's Field opposite the old farmhouse, drilling down to 235 feet. Alan Champion, a gentleman to the last, not only raised no protest against the plans, he also chose to sell Vale Farm to the Water Board in 1975 rather than await compulsory purchase. He and Winifred moved to Sturry with Averil, who married and left home just six months later. The Vale Farm land was rented out to Vincent Brealy. When Les

Moran and Fred and Bill Jordan were made redundant by the sale of the farm, Les went to work for Vincent Brealy and Bill Jordan accepted a job with the Water Board. For around ten years after they had left, the Champions continued to keep Hereford bullocks on land near the fields known as "Robsack" and "Little Gains", due to their poor yield.

Although there has been much negative publicity over the years about the effect of the reservoir plans and the uncertain fate of Vale Farm, there were also two positive events that have helped to preserve it for posterity. The first was in 1975, around the time of the sale, when the area around Vale Farm was chosen as the location for the making of the film "The Prince And The Pauper". The second was in the mid-1980's, when the Museum for Kent Rural Life received a special cash grant that enabled them to buy Vale Farm's eighteenth-century barn from the Water Board. The old structure was painstakingly dismantled and then carefully rebuilt at the open-air museum at Cobtree Manor Park, near Maidstone. When the completed building was ready for public viewing Alan Champion visited the museum, and he was photographed inside the barn, alongside the displays of antique farming implements and machinery that now replaced the potatoes that were stored in it during its working life at Vale Farm: a farmer and his farm building, both now retired from active service.

If the theorists are correct, it is comforting to think that the fifty years of the Champions' tenure at Vale Farm have somehow been absorbed into the fabric of the old barn, and that whatever the future holds for the Broad Oak Valley, an important part of its history will live on long after all living memory of it is lost.

Mayton Farm and the Imhofs

By P.D and M.A. Crampton

Early Years on the Farm

By the time the Imhof family bought Mayton Farm in 1955, no trace of the old Tudor farmhouse remained above the ground. Like so many other such notable buildings, it had been requisitioned during the Second World War, and never recovered from the experience. During this period, Les Moran, who worked for the

Champions at Vale Farm, used to help out at Mayton whenever the previous owner Bill Taylor needed extra hands at threshing time. He remembers how he and the other farm workers used to go inside the old farmhouse to eat their lunch. By then, the old wallpaper had fallen away to reveal a layer of newspaper pasted on in the nineteenth century. Compared with today's tabloids, these must have made interesting lunchtime reading. After falling into a state of uninhabitable disrepair, demolition was the kindest option and the old building was despatched in 1953. The house has been commemorated in photographs and also in a drawing by Roger Higham, based on an old photograph, and on which he has noted:

"Jetty House circa 1570-1630 from a photograph in the possession of F Neaves, Leopards Head Garage, Sturry".

In the late 1950s, even the foundations of the lost house were dug out and used to repair the ruts in Mayton Lane between the farm and Langton Lodge. Although no structural remains of the building survive today, it is said that the brickwork from the original well can still be found within the old farmyard area.

When the Imhofs arrived at Mayton, a newly married John Imhof moved into Apsley Lodge, a mid nineteenth-century shooting lodge, which stood on the opposite side of Mayton Lane. His brother Michael and sister Anne initially shared a caravan that was parked outside. A new farmhouse was constructed a year after their arrival by the building firm Else, who had also been responsible for the new Vale Farm house. Michael and Anne moved in to the new house with their parents, Ernest and Ethel, until Michael went away to University, and Anne married. Michael would return to work on the farm during his holidays from University, and one of the rooms at the farmhouse was always known as "Michael's Room". Both brothers were members of Canterbury Rugby Team.

In 1956, a son Robert was born to John Imhof and his wife. They later had a daughter Deryl in 1960 and another daughter, Rhiannon, in 1975. The name Imhof had initially caused a little concern in the Broad Oak Valley. This was the time of the Cold War, and there was speculation that they could be Russian spies, a suspicion reinforced by the discovery of a glove, with the name "Imhof" written inside. It had, in fact, been mislaid by an aunt, whilst out on a walk in the valley.

At the time of their taking over the farm, the main farm buildings on the south side of Mayton Lane formed three sides of a square. On the west side was a hay barn and implement shed, a cow byre on the north side and thatched barns, which were said to have survived from Sidney Cooper's tenure, on the south side. The slate roof of the hay barn may have replaced an earlier thatch. In the middle of the yard was a midden. Behind the implement shed were sand pits where badgers used to have their setts.

The Imhofs carried out many improvements to the farm. Among the first of these was the replacement of the corrugated-iron back wall of the byre with breeze blocks, and the installation of a silage clamp parallel to the implement shed. In 1963 a large double-roofed Dutch barn was constructed. A thatched building that stood to the left of the new silage clamp was removed at the same time. Ernest Imhof erected a brooder house and incubator shed in 1960 on the south side of the yard. They were used for storage after 1966 when the Imhofs gave up keeping chickens. The introduction of a vaccine for Brucella necessitated the building of isolation sheds, to house the animals awaiting treatment. These were put up in 1969, again by Ernest Imhof.

In 1967, John Imhof demonstrated an admirable early attempt at recycling when he used scrap metal from a dismantled pylon to construct low-loaders for use on the farm. The Shelford Farm-based pylon had become redundant when land slippage necessitated a new replacement. John Imhof, who assisted in its dismantling, took a camera with him and used the opportunity to record several aerial photographs. Unwittingly, he was recording a view of the Broad Oak valley that was soon to be threatened with obliteration.

The most imposing of all the Mayton Farm buildings was the nineteenth century oast house standing on the north side of Mayton Lane. Mayton had long ceased to be a hop farm, when the Imhofs acquired the oast. At first they used part of the building to store calf-nuts. Later, they produced homemade cattle feed by milling their own barley and mixing it with Soya oil. Ernest Imhof re-made the large double doors to the oast, beyond which a huge grain pit was dug. Trailers loaded with grain would reverse back through the doors and tip the grain into the pit. Inside the oast was an old winnowing machine, converted to electricity by John Imhof, who also erected two huge grain bins. At the eastern end of the oast was a diesel tank. There was another room, behind the old calf-nut store, that was used for egg cleaning.

The wooden shed next to the oast house was used initially as a milking parlour. The calves were housed in the east end of the building and the milking herd in the west end. The cows stood in stalls in the shed, and the milking machine would move from stall to stall. A Petter engine, housed in a nearby shed next to the churn stand, powered the machine, which was connected to it by a vacuum line. There was a room between the shed and the oast that was used as a dairy. As the size of the herd increased, the byre was divided into three, by gates, and the cows were brought up in batches to be milked. Later a new milking parlour was built for the Imhofs by Messrs Else, who had also carried out the breezeblock work on the cow byre. In the angle between

the cow byre and the hay barn was an isolation box used for tuberculin test reactors. Deryl Imhof remembers one cow that had to be kept apart from the herd whilst its test results were double-checked. It was kept on a chain, and it took to following John Imhof. Eventually it preferred the company of humans to the other cows!

Facilities at Mayton Farm were fairly basic. Water had originally been drawn from a spring in a field below Mayton farm. Years ago it would have been carried up to the farm in buckets on a yoke, milkmaid-style. When the Imhofs took over, there was a pump house on the edge of the wood behind the barn, upon which was a red light that would glow when the water level was low. In the winter the frozen pipes had to be dug out and thawed. Soon after their arrival at Mayton, the Imhofs converted a hilltop wind-pump to electricity, to raise water to the farm. Until the mid-1970s, when the Water Board became responsible for the testing of the water, drinking water was delivered to the farm in large bottles. Following the first test, the Imhofs were informed that the water was fit to drink by anyone who was neither under the age of two, or pregnant. As a result, mains water was installed.

Photograph by Paul Crampton

Datestone at Apsley Lodge, Mayton

Apsley Lodge

The two-bedroomed Apsley Lodge was rather on the small side for a family of four, and although it had both running water and a bathroom, the only toilet was outside. There was a north-facing pantry that was so cold, no fridge was ever needed there. The front door to the property was never used and the passage to it instead used to accommodate bookcases. As well as the outside toilet, there was another outhouse that was used as a coal-hole and for storage. Deryl and Robert were not allowed to venture inside. The wedge-shaped garden also contained several trees, including a large Morello cherry, later blown down in a storm.

By March 1965, the Imhof children were sharing the back bedroom. Around the same time, bootlace fungus was discovered behind the wallpaper and plaster of the bedroom walls. This, together with the need for Deryl and Robert to have their own rooms, led to an application being made to Bridge-Blean Council for a replacement dwelling. After an initial reluctance to agree to a new building, an inspection of Apsley Lodge was carried out and the necessary permission then followed. The new bungalow was constructed by the building firm Else, on the opposite side of Mayton Lane to Apsley Lodge. It was finally completed in

1970, and the Imhofs then moved out of Apsley Lodge. They dismantled their old home themselves, with even Deryl and Robert lending a hand by removing the peg tiles from the roof. Their father paid them one penny for each tile they removed in one piece. Like its previously demolished neighbour Mayton Farm house, the rubble remains were used to level out the rutted Mayton Lane. The stone bearing the name of Apsley Lodge, and date of construction - 1859 - was carefully removed. It was propped against the front wall of its successor, officially called just "Apsley", where in time it gradually disintegrated. The plot where the old house stood was later used as an enclosure for calves.

The Coming of the Reservoir

There can be little doubt that, had the reservoir scheme been known to the Imhofs in 1955, it would definitely have influenced their decision to buy Mayton Farm. When the plans were finally announced, John Imhof immediately set about gathering support from other land owners for a joint approach to be made to a London-based legal firm, who could help them prepare for the Water Board's purchase offers. A fourteen-year-old Deryl Imhof was allowed to attend meetings about the reservoir scheme, held at Broad Oak village hall, on the condition that she did not speak at them.

The Water Board bought Mayton Farm in 1974. The following year, John Imhof, who had considered, and then decided against, becoming a tenant farmer, bought another farm at Carmarthen in Wales. He continued to rent farmland at both Mayton and Blaxland on a yearly licence. He used the land to grow arable crops, the revenue from which was used to support the Welsh farm, where the Mayton dairy herd now resided. John Imhof, assisted by farm worker Brian Lawrence, achieved the massive relocation process by transporting three loads of fourteen animals each, every day for a total of three weeks. Arthur Garner, the Mayton Farm cowman from 1960, went with the herd to see that they were settled in to their new home. For a time, he also considered moving to Wales, but instead stayed in Kent and retired to Whitstable. John Imhof continued to commute between Carmarthen and Kent, and would bring back young calves to be reared at Blaxland.

The Pop Festival Plans

In the early 1970s, students were squatting in many of the properties that had been both bought and boarded up by the Water Board. Eventually, the arrangement was made official and these houses were let out to the University. In due course, people who were not students also began to move in, and gradually a new community began to form, which became something of a microcosm of alternative lifestyles. From this developed an idea in 1976 that the Broad Oak valley might be the ideal location for a pop festival, presumably inspired by the successes at Woodstock and the Isle of Wight. The advanced billing for this "People's Free Festival" was sufficient to trigger a huge police operation in the valley.

The Imhofs were informed that all their windows and doors had to be securely locked – as were all the residents in Mayton and Barnet Lanes - as the police would be powerless to either eject squatters who had taken over an unsecured building, or to treat such an intrusion as a break-in. All roads to the valley were barricaded, and it was genuinely feared that everything within a five mile radius would be completely trashed. Two Water Board-owned JCBs were based at Mayton Farm; one had a wide end and was to be used if any festival supporter caused an obstruction by lying in the road. It could scoop them up, along with some earth, and they would not suffer any injury.

Mayton Manor, demolished in 1953

Photograph by kind permission of Brian Stewart

Fire Officers advised the Imhofs to burn any stubble in the fields that surrounded the buildings, and any unnecessary equipment was moved away from the valley for safekeeping. Deryl Imhof recalls that Tom Castle, (whose aunt Vera Matthews lived at "Brambles" Farm) and his men, arrived one Sunday and removed a lot of their equipment for them. Police officers were stationed at "Apsley" during the time that the festival was due to be held, and during periods of inactivity they would play cricket in the area between the new bungalow and the farmhouse. John Imhof provided the teas.

In the event, the festival did not go ahead, at least in the Broad Oak valley. Instead, a festival of sorts was held at Seasalter, on the very day that the long hot summer of 1979 was at last broken by a violent thunderstorm.

Mayton Memories

Growing up in the Broad Oak Valley has left Deryl Imhof with many fond memories of both the area and its inhabitants. Her childhood friends included Lesley Tharp from Blaxland Farm and Arthur Garner's children. Jack Collard, known locally as "Thatcher Jack", used to make corn dollies for the young Deryl.

John Imhof intrigued his daughter with stories of lost houses, one of which was said to have stood at Burnt Oak, just beyond Langton Lodge. Deryl later found some old pottery there. Michael Imhof found a Stone Age implement in a corner of a field near the rickyard at Mayton; knappings found in the same area would suggest that the tool was actually made on site. It is now in the Royal Museum in Canterbury. Below the farmhouse, earthworks were visible that might have been the remains of a prehistoric settlement site. It was in that area that John Imhof found what appeared to be an old sickle.

Final Years

By 1978, Deryl was studying for her A Levels at the Simon Langton Girls' School and she stayed on at Mayton until she had finished her exams. John Imhof, still commuting between the Welsh farm and Mayton, was aghast to discover that Deryl had been walking alone through the woods, and then all the way to Greenhill, to attend Sea Rangers meetings. Deryl pointed out that she found this preferable to braving the drug addicts in Mayton Lane and the drunks at the Broad Oak pubs!

For a time, John Imhof considered returning to Kent and running just an arable farm. He went as far as agreeing to a sale on the Carmarthen farm, but it fell through. When the yearly licence for the Mayton and Blaxland farms reached its expiry date in 1981, he did not renew it. Vincent Brealy took it over instead. In that same year John Imhof also took the decision to give up farming altogether. This was prompted by a fall in the price of cattle, and the fact that he was missing out on the childhood years of his youngest daughter Rhiannon. He quickly found a buyer for the Carmarthen farm, and he and his family relocated to North Wales.

Only five years later, whilst on a trip with Rhiannon to the local swimming pool, John Imhof died suddenly from a heart attack. He was only fifty.

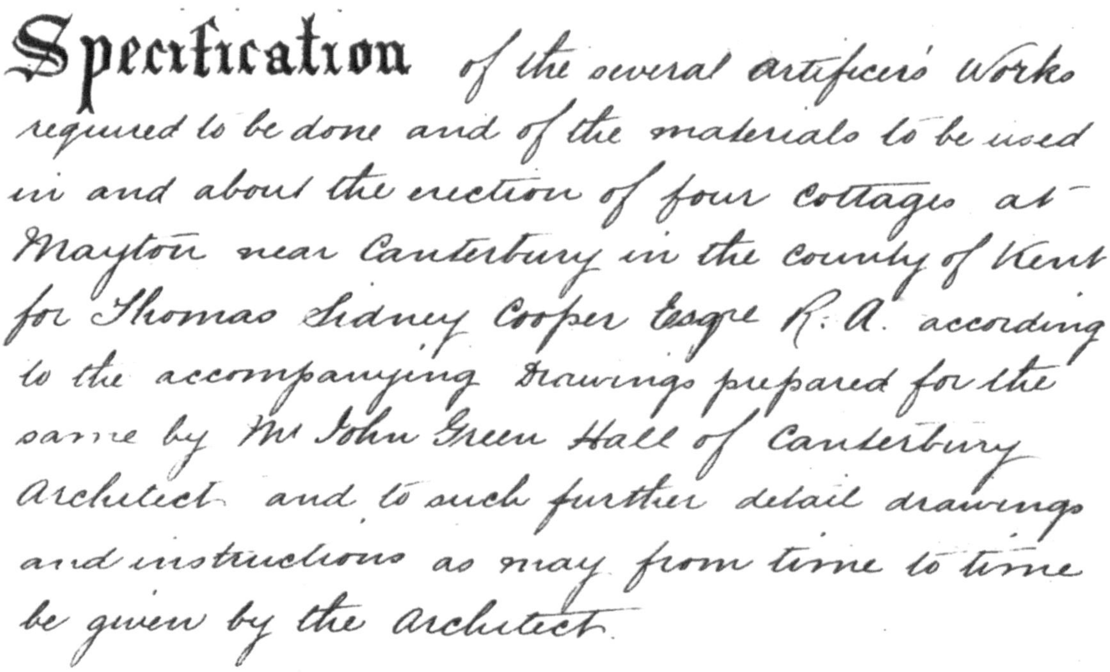

Specification of the several artificers' Works required to be done and of the materials to be used in and about the erection of four cottages at Mayton near Canterbury in the county of Kent for Thomas Sidney Cooper Esqre R.A. according to the accompanying drawings prepared for the same by Mr John Green Hall of Canterbury Architect and to such further detail drawings and instructions as may from time to time be given by the architect.

reproduced by kind permission of Kenneth Westwood

Extract from the agreement and specification for the building of T.Sidney Cooper's cottages at Mayton from the Kenneth J.Westwood Collection. Kenneth Westwood is the author of *Thomas Sidney Cooper – His life and Work* (Volume 1,*Master of Lithography*, pub Wilson Hunt, 1991. Further volumes in preparation).

The police blockade at the top of Mayton Lane before the proposed Pop Festival

Photograph by Michael Waterman

COUNTDOWN TO A POP FESTIVAL, August 1976

By Heather Stennett

Gleaned from local and national newspaper reports in a scrap book kept by Rosie Cullen (nee Jackson)

Friday 13th

The lack of water in the south east convinced Canterbury's MP Mr David Crouch that a Broad Oak reservoir was necessary. His support for the scheme was made public while speaking in a debate about the Drought Bill. His comments were recorded in the Kentish Gazette. This information was cause for concern for protesters fighting the controversial plans, but more bad news was to follow.

Monday 16th

The Peoples' Free Festival committee announced that Broad Oak had been chosen after abandoning earlier plans to stage a Festival at the old Tangmere RAF station, near Chichester Sussex, following local protests. Mid Kent Water Co had not been asked for permission to use any of their land and they reported that 'their tenants knew nothing about a festival, only rumours'.

Wednesday 18th

High Court Judge, Mr Justice Slade, barred the organisers from holding the free pop festival in Sussex. Four of the organisers gave their undertaking not to stage a pop festival in Sussex or Broad Oak but a fifth organiser Mr John Pollard claimed that the Festival would go ahead on August 27th on land in the valley at Broad Oak 'We are going to Broad Oak valley whatever the Water Board says. It's our summer holiday and we won't be messed around'. Kent police pledged to act in strength to prevent unlawful intrusion and deal firmly with any breaches of the law which may occur.

(The Guardian 19-08-1976)

Friday 20th

Mr Justice Slade, High Court Judge granted a temporary ban on the organising of a free pop festival. The order was granted to Mid Kent Water Co., the University of Kent, and three farmers

Vincent Brealy, Gerald and Ralph Stevens. The order was made against Mr John Kevin Pollard and the other 7 or 8 organisers. The order was effective until Wednesday 25th. It was reported that there was fear of damage to crops particularly 'hops soon to be harvested.' (Mr Charles Aldous, counsel for the Plaintiffs) to which one of the organisers replied that there were no crops on the site.

The organisers expected about 10000 fans to arrive. Police leave was cancelled and a special incident room was set up at Canterbury Police Station. City Council Planning Committee gave their full support to Mid Kent Water Co.

(The Times 21-08-1976)

Mr Jex Cole, of Ewell, Surrey, was one of the organisers who gave details about the proposed festival. It was planned to have portable stages on which 150 groups would play for nothing, using electricity from portable generators. He stressed that it was not a pop festival but a free festival where there would be alternative technology, theatre groups, poets and free food stalls and suchlike. The organisers did not have any financial backing but income from food sellers and stallholders on the site would cover costs. (Kentish Gazette 20-08-1976)

NFU representative Mr Tony Elliot visited the valley and said that reports 'that the land was unused were totally wrong'. 45 acres of potatoes, estimated value £40000+ in fields next to the site had been grown by Vincent Brealy. The potatoes would take up to 12 weeks before they had set, and been harvested ready for storage. There were storages of baled hay and straw and apples of unknown tonnage were still on the trees. (Kent Herald and Canterbury News 24-08-1976)

Emergency services would be on alert, worries about 'food poisoning, sunburn, problems with alcohol and other form of tranquilising' were among the warnings given by Dr Harvey, the Health Advisor to the City Council. The vice chairman of Sturry

Parish council Michael Kent voiced concerns over noise and the lack of facilities. Kent County councillor John Heddle was concerned about problems of vandalism, hooliganism and health hazards for local residents.
(Kentish Gazette 20-08-1976)

Mr Jex Cole – there are lots of fields there not being used at present, although I don't know much about the site because I haven't been there.

We have worked closely with Lord Melchett, who is the chairman of the Governments Working Group to review Public Police on Pop Festivals and it was him that mentioned Broad Oak when we suggested Tangmere
(Kentish Gazette 20 -8 – 76)

Saturday 21st

The first fan arrived, spending the night in a sleeping bag near the proposed festival site. Just after 7am Sunday he was found by Mid Kent Water Co. regular patrols. He was woken up, told he was not allowed to stay, and he left.

Monday 23rd

A dozen farmers, members of Canterbury NFU, went to Blaxland farm to move 80 tons/2000 bales of straw from a barn. The bales were owned by John Imhof and they were taken 5 miles away, for safe storage. Organisers said that the festival was still defiantly on. All Police leave was cancelled over the Bank Holiday, Broad Oak Hall was used as temporary Police station, normal activities and meetings in the Hall were cancelled. 2 radio aerials were erected next to village hall to keep mobile patrols in touch with Supt. Doug Fenn, Head of Canterbury Sub-division. Police were billeted at Howe barracks. By this time deep trenches, high earth walls and barbed wire fences had been put across field entrances. £500 was authorised from the rates to erect barriers. The main plan of campaign was aimed at making it physically impossible for the organisers to get any vehicles into the valley. All livestock had been removed.

Tuesday 24th

Mrs Hazel McCabe, C.C.C. Tyler Hill representative, at a Public meeting about the reservoir, told the meeting that Mid Kent Water Co. and C.C.C. were doing everything that was legally and humanly possible to prevent the festival from taking place.

By now the Festival was well and truly in the public domain. Articles appeared in all the National newspapers and Television News reports. The event was being broadcast on Radio Luxembourg and leaflets/fliers distributed at Knebworth music festival informed festival goers of the Broad Oak event. Bands such as Hawkwind, LSD Band, Gong, Half Human Band and Arthur Brown were mentioned as being expected to appear.

Wednesday 25th

The Guardian Newspaper appealed to fans to give this one a miss….amid the real risk of fire.

Police, Farmers and water board were keeping in radio contact and plans were being drawn up to run air patrols to spot fans.

The Temporary Injunction was renewed in the High Court for one day, banning an eight day event, the free pop festival. The Golden Lion closed. Regulars were staying away. 'Without regulars we were just supporting the people coming to the festival so we decided to close down' J.McLoughlin was quoted as saying in the Kentish Gazette.

Thursday 26th

High Court Judge Mr Justice Slade banned 5 men; Mr Cole, Dr Pollard, Mr MacDonald, Mr Brookham and Mr Nightingale from organising the proposed festival. Festival Welfare workers Mr Donald Aitken and Miss Victoria Strangroome were ordered to keep off the site unless they had written consent from the owners.

Fear of clashes between Police and Fans was growing, Fans begin to converge on the area. They were turned away by roadblocks and Police with dogs.

The Guardian reported that 'Acres of fields are being sprayed with repellent dung! Cultivators were run over stubble in fields to reduce the fire risk.

The two Public Houses were closed until further notice but Post Office Village Stores remained open. Water Co. officials were angry with about 16 fans who had already pitched camp in the garden of Little Mayton, a university-let cottage. They had arrived about a week earlier and officials had no way of evicting them. Most fans were expected to stay away but concern was voiced about the possible invasion of youngsters only interested in a clash with the authorities.

Mr David Crouch has written to the Home Secretary seeking an assurance that a Government working Party on Free Pop Festivals did not advise the fans to go to Broad Oak.
(The Guardian, 26-8-76)

Friday 27th

The Times reported that the slow trickle of fans was outnumbered by the 250 policemen and dogs. The Police were guarding the 3 main routes. Fans arriving went peacefully away again. 24 hour patrols by 200 police checking on each and everyone's identity. Water Board employees were strategically placed in the narrow lanes. Mr Collard, the Water Board's Divisional Engineer warned that 1000 acres of farmland are in danger.

Quotes

- *'The scene looked more like a Police Training exercise than a Hippy Music Festival'* (The Times)
- *'There are too many coppers here. There is nothing wrong with the few fans arriving here. They don't want to fight and nor do we'*
- *'I'm not as apprehensive as some people. As a pop festival it would be a good thing. It's been an over reaction'*
- *'It's just a bit of life and its free - there's nothing in Canterbury'*
- *'What is building up is a confrontation mentally on both sides'*
(The Guardian)

There were showers of rain in the morning. Fans were reported to be sheltering under the tree in front of the Royal Oak. It was reported that Police searches had led to more than a dozen arrests for alleged drug offences.
(The Guardian 28-08-1976)

2 wigwams were erected in a field near Seasalter, this signalled a new centre for the People's Free Festival '76 and scores of fans made their way to the new site.

The barricades remained at Broad Oak amid concerns the new venue was a hoax.

It rained.

Village Voices - 3

Edited extract from an interview with Sheila Moran and Dot Gammon (now aged 75) by Heather Stennett (2006)

HS: Tell me what it was like when you were young. . .

SM: Everybody knew everybody else it seemed all so friendly then. We never even thought about locking our doors. The neighbours were neighbours. I remember Mrs Bacon (your grandmother) she lived in the council houses. She used to go and lay people out when they died, you would never get that now, and another thing used to be if anybody passed away, everybody pulled their curtains and stood still and waited. I remember going down to the small school and if we saw a coffin come down we just stood like that to attention till it had gone. It was so different in those days.

DG: Yes, you respected people, didn't you?

SM: It was so friendly, times have changed so much. I mean I don't know hardly anybody in the village now

HS: You both worked in the fields together didn't you. Now, let's go back to the early days of hop picking. Did you go hop picking?

SM: Oh yes, I had to go hop picking to get my winter uniform for school. We had to sit and pick. We used to go off about 6 o'clock in the morning and we used to go through, past the Mayton cottages through that field and it was so wet and damp with dew.

DG: To Tyler Hill.

SM: When we got there we was wet through and it was about 10 o'clock before we dried out.

DG: Well you couldn't see half the time because it was so misty going across the fields and the old bullocks were out in the fields, and you were half asleep but you had woken up by the time you had gotten there. I know we used to get up very early. It was lovely dinner time when you could boil a kettle on the wood fire and make a cup of tea with condensed milk

HS: Did you used to have to make your own fire or was there a communal fire?

DG: No – we had to make our own

SM: There was a lot of huts up there that people from London come down to stay…… that was their holiday, and they was there for all the hop picking. I think they used to have riotous times in the evening and all that

HS: How did the locals get on with these 'foreigners' from London?

SM: Very well I think

HS: The kids did they all play together?

SM: Well I can't remember

DG: I don't think they were allowed to go off and play not until you had picked your bushel

SM: No you weren't

HS: So there wasn't really time for mischief

SM: Sometimes we were picking too many leaves. So we had to stand and pick all the leaves out. They were really hard days but we never thought anything of it

HS: Can you remember the name of the farm you went to?

SM: Whiting's?

DG: Mr Stephens then it was Mr Philpott was the foreman there – in charge

SM: There again it was a really big concern but they don't have hop pickers now, they have these machines, it's all so different. I remember these men used to go around on these wooden things walking

HS: Stilts

SM: To tie the hops up. I suppose that's all done by machines now

DG: Years ago when we were children in the village there used to be the oilman used to come into the village. His name was Mr Gammon – Albert, I think - and he used to sell everything, something.

SM: What did they used to call him though, his nickname?

DG: I don't know but he came from the Stodmarsh Road but he sold paraffin, candles, matches, vinegar. Everything, something he sold and he used to call out didn't he, and we used to go and get whatever we wanted. He used to come every week.

HS: There was the 3 shops and then there was these travelling salesmen. Who else used to come?

DG: There used to be a tinker come round selling buttons and cottons, wasn't there? Then there used to be a

couple of Indians used to come round selling

SM: Well I remember no one would answer the door to them because they were frightened of them. In those days any one of that colour. . .

DG: He come to my mum and she got these silk pillowcases with elephants on and my mum took a liking to them so she had 2 and she ordered 2 more and my dad – he wasn't at home on that particular day. But anyhow the man came back in a fortnight and he brought these two cushions over, and he came in the gate but I don't know what my dad said to him but the poor man went and anyhow my mum had a go at my dad and she went after the man and she bought her cushions. He said something in a foreign language.

SM: They were resented in those days those people

DG: They were but she wanted them cushion covers.

SM: And then on a Sunday there used to be this man come round and there used to be a bike with a great big basket in the front – Ron used to have one delivering years ago – and he used to bring fish round. Cockles and mussels and shrimps and winkles and we always used to have shrimps and winkles on a Sunday, and then we used

Nellie and Winifred Glover and bridesmaid Linda Glover outside 31 Sweechgate Cottages dressed for the wedding of Margaret Brickwood and Arthur Glover in 1952.

Photograph by courtesy of Lisa Haines

to have to fight for a big pin because the one who got the biggest pin could pick these winkles out much quicker than ones that had got small ones. Of course then there was the man who used to come and put the lights on every night, Mr Issacs, on the bike. He had a son, Trevor

DG: I remember that plain as anything

SM: Even the council houses used to have gas mantles. They was always breaking

DG: In the blackout we had to have blackout curtains didn't we? We were evacuated weren't we?

HS: You were evacuated?

DG: We were. We lived up the alley and there was a landmine went in Mrs Goodburn's house near where my Mum's house was here.

HS: So for a fortnight you weren't allowed in your house.

DG: And Cecil was away and he come home and they wouldn't let him into the village so he cut back because Mum and them was away because of Mrs Pout's having a landmine. Dad was there because he was a Home Guard and Cecil cut back and he came back between the Pout's and Broad Oak House, it was a Cherry Orchard then, and he got home that way.

SM: The first time the siren went off at home Mum was absolutely petrified. She was so worried she got all the newspapers she could, wet them down and we used to have air vents in the bedroom and she went upstairs and she stuffed them full of this wet paper 'cos she thought there was going to be gas

DG: I remember when war broke out and that aeroplane went down over Nora's woods. It was Sunday lunchtime and it went straight over our house and landed in the woods it was low and then there was the Blitz in Canterbury those planes that came over when Bill was a baby. We thought it was a band coming along the road. It was the aeroplane firing all the bullets when the bus got hit down Calcott, and my Mum was getting the washing in and I shouted "come on in, Mum" 'cos of the aeroplane.

SM: We used to stand and watch them going over to London to bomb. But it was alright all the time they were going over. It was when they were coming back 'cos they were intercepted and they used to drop their bombs anywhere to get back. It was quite frightening.

DG: We got used to it. When we thought that there was going to be an invasion when war first broke out Mr Lawrence had all his wagons across the road down by Sweechgate in case the Germans came 'cos they thought they would come across from France to Dover and they would be here in no time so they barricaded the road, didn't they? They put all the wagons between Sweechgate bungalow [the toll-gate cottage] and Mollie's house. [Exeter Villa]. They put them across the road

SM: As soon as the siren went off old Mr Collingwood who lived opposite, he used to come out with his tin hat on - he had a stretcher, too, and he used to prop it against the front door and then he used to walk up and down the road with this rattle. Well, I don't know what anybody thought they was going to do.

Once they [the Germans] got over they would be here!

DG: Twice a week I had to go to Sturry to pick up the accumulator for the wireless. When I was coming up the hill at 10 to 6 that night when the landmine dropped with the train going through and I saw all the sparks going up. I was with Violet Jones she had come up with me. That's when the landmine dropped in Sturry and all those people were killed. We just got to the school. When my Dad was at home if the news was on we had to be dead quiet, you wasn't allowed to talk. My father was in the army. He's always been an army man. He went to an army school and then he joined up. His first job was as a bugler boy. Then he was in the Marines and in 1939 he joined up … He was working over at Amos's in Littlebourne Road at Bekesbourne with my uncle and auntie, he had to get a job over there and my mum had to work. There was me and Denny and Eva, Ted was a baby, and this letter came that morning saying that my Dad had got to join up in the Garrison Theatre in Canterbury in Whitehall at 2 o'clock that afternoon so we did no more and we walked all the way to Littlebourne, and found him, and told him. He got on his bike and he came home. By the time we got home he was gone. He was decorated for his services, he was in the SAS but he never told you what he had done, after the war he worked at the barracks in the stores. He did all the books for the Bat and Trap players at one time, too.

Back row: Dave Carman, Geoff Jones, George Harvey, Maurice Collingwoood, A N Other, Richard Fordyce
Front row: Peter Townsend, Colin Kennett, Trevor Skewis, Roger Williams, A? Dobson

Photograph by courtesy of The Kentish Gazette

Fund - Raising, 1928

Broad Oak Fete in Aid of Recreation Hut

The long cherished dream of a recreation hut for the village of Broad Ok is now happily well on the way to being realised, for the building is actually in course of erection. The funds have been raised by various means and on Wednesday a fete, organised by the Hut Committee, was held by kind permission of Mr E.J.Port, in the meadow adjoining Goose Farm. The success of the event may be gauged from the fact that over 500 tickets were sold before the day.

The various stalls and sideshows were supervised as follows: Garden produce: Miss E. Goodburn, Home Workers' Stall: Mrs Hall, Miss Goodburn, Sweets: Mrs Coulson. Teas: Mrs Cackett and a large number of helpers. Shooting for Goal: Mr T. Potten. Dart Games: Miss Collingwood, Miss Keem. Balloon Bursting: Mr R. Collingwood, Spinning Jenny: Mr N. Rowland. Coconuts: Mr Lloyd, Tons of Money: Mr Osharn. Lucky Tree: Miss M.Port. Bowling for Pig: Messrs Cooper and Patterson. Penny in a basket: Mrs P. Boker. Treasure Garden: Mr F. Rowland. Ice creams: Miss Lloyd, Miss E.Culver. Competitions: Mrs Port, Mrs Holness, Miss Collingwood and Mr C. Goodburn. (The turkey was given by Mr G. Lawrence). Devil amongst the Tailors: Mr F.Hall.

The O.K. Minstrels' Orchestra provided music in the evening and for dancing on the green. A confetti battle caused great fun and hilarity, while the fire-fighting display by the Broad Oak Boys' Own Fire Brigade, under the captaincy of Master E. Port – who is following in his father's footsteps – showed that the youngsters were quite "all there" when it came to "four man wet" and one man drill.

During the day the harvest was reaped, F. Cackett, J.Patterson and R. Lucas, who, in a charming variety of headgear, perambulated the district with a melodious barrel organ.

The committee of which Mr E Port was chairman and organiser, Mr R.Collingwood, the hon secretary, and Mr F. Cackett. hon treasurer, are to be congratulated on the success of the day.

From The Kentish Gazette

Broad Oak Football Team
Back row: Peter Townsend, Colin Kennett, Michael Wells, Maurice Collingwood, Colin Gow, Dave Carman,
Front row: Terry Jones, William Harwood, Geoff Jones, Trevor Croxton

Broad Oak Village Hall

By Jackie Moran

In the mid -1920's, several residents of Broad Oak Village agreed that a Village Hall was needed for the local community. A steering committee was formed to organise fund-raising and Mr. E. J. Port (Goose Farm), Mr. A. Hadlow (Sweechgate Stores), Mr.R Collingwood and Mr. F. Cacket, were in the forefront of this first committee. Land was acquired in Shalloak Road and in 1928, the wooden village hall was built by Mr. Gates, a builder from Herne Village.

The Hall was used for organised parties, celebrations, dances, whist drives and by various groups and organisations until 1939, when it was requisitioned by the Kent County Council. From 1939 to 1945, the Hall served as a canteen for army personnel (the Royal Welsh Fusiliers) stationed at Broad Oak Farm. Up until this time gas was used to heat, light and power the Hall. In 1946, electricity was installed for lighting only.

The responsibility for the management of the Hall was returned to the villagers in 1946, when a Watch Committee was formed and a written constitution, with guidance .from the Charity Commissioners, set out. This stated that no religious or political

meetings could be held in the Hall and that all Committee members must be residents of Broad Oak Village. In later years this was amended by the Commissioners to permit certain organisations using the Hall on a regular basis, to be represented on the Committee. This first Constitution also required 3 local residents to act as Trustees. In later years this was also amended by the Commissioners, and the serving Management Committee are now also the Hall Trustees.

The activities in the Hall continued to flourish, with Committee organised functions such as Christmas parties for the elderly and young children, Jumble sales, dances, whist drives and film shows. Catering for the parties and for many local weddings, was organised by Mrs Mollie Rose and her willing band of local lady helpers. A Monday Lunch Club for the Over 60's was organised by the W .R. V.S.

In the late 1970' s, the outside toilets and existing kitchen were demolished and a brick extension was constructed adjoining the main hall. This consisted of a fitted kitchen, ladies and gentlemen's toilets, a storeroom and a committee room. The Committee was

Photograph by courtesy of the Kentish Gazette

Members of the Committee of the Broad Oak Hall in November, 1989: Denis Hope, Michael Kent, Jackie Moran,(Chairman) Janet McKenzie, Marian Hope, Irene Miller, Philip Moore, Pat Owen, Ted Todd and Jonathan Clark.

chaired firstly by Michael Kent of Shalloak Road, and then by Mr.Edward Todd of Sweechgate and the necessary finance was raised by local fund-raising, including a 'Buy a Brick' Appeal and grant aid from the Department of Education & Science, Canterbury City Council and Sturry Parish Council.

From 1970 more organisations had started to hire the Hall on a regular basis. These included the newly formed Broad Oak Playgroup and Broad Oak W.I, Keep Fit Classes, a local Majorette Group and a male Fitness Club.

By 1985 the population of the village of Broad Oak had increased considerably and it was becoming clear that the Hall, with its suspended wooden floor, was no longer suitable for modern musical entertainment and physical activities. Justifiable complaints from nearby residents resulted in restrictions having to be made on the usage of the Hall. It was clear that a new building was needed if local residents were to be able to continue to use their Hall.

In 1986 plans were drawn up by Mr. Terry Edwards of Shalloak Road, for a new brick and timber clad building. These were submitted to the Canterbury City Council and passed. Applications were made to the City and County Councils for Grant Aid on two occasions. Each time the Kent County Council refused the application. The City Council was willing to help financially. The possibility of improving the existing wooden building was discussed with the City Council but the Committee believed that a new Hall was the only satisfactory solution. In 1989, a further application for grant-aid was made. This time the application was backed by a signed petition and letters of support from local residents. The application was successful, but the Committee had to raise 25% of the total cost. This was done by fundraising and pledges from local residents. The City Council gave a further 25% and the remaining 50% was given by the Kent County Council.

The work of removing the wooden Hall and the building of the new Hall was started in June 1989. The builder was Mr. Andrew Batt from Westbere. The Hall was taken down and removed by an organisation known as the Fifth Trust (from Barham), to be used as a workshop for young persons with certain disabilities. When the

Trust removed the roof timbers a signature of the 1928 builder was discovered and this they framed and presented to the Hall Committee.

The new Hall was officially opened on 14th October, 1989 by Cllr. David Pentin ~ and a celebratory event was held for villagers and all who had helped to make the 'Dream' a reality.

1n 2004, the Hall had to comply with the Government legislation concerning disabled persons using the building. A concrete ramp for access had been installed in 1989, but suitable toilet facilities were necessary. The storeroom was converted to provide this facility and was paid for by applying and being accepted for Grant Aid from the Brett Environmental Trust.

Broad Oak Hall has continued to be a much cherished asset by the Village. From the early days when locals would ask 'Are you going up the Hut tonight?' to the present day, it has shown that those who had the forethought to fund-raise and build the original Hall, knew what our Village needed. Residents of Broad Oak - please remember it is 'OUR VILLAGE HALL' and may it continue to serve the needs of our Village for at least another 65 years.

Broad Oak Hut 1928-1989

The Blean Woods a wildlife haven

A history of coppicing

Situated to the north, north-west of the Broad Oak village, West Blean and Thornden Wood represent 489 hectares of semi-natural ancient woodland part of the much more extensive Blean woodland complex. Ancient woods are by definition areas where trees have grown continuously since before 1600. These woods usually have a higher conservation value than more recently planted woodlands.

West Blean and Thornden Wood are currently managed as a nature reserve by the Kent Wildlife Trust and form an important part of a wider conservation jigsaw, linking the Blean Woods National Nature Reserve in the west with East Blean Wood in the east. Some 40% of the reserve is a dense conifer plantation and 40% is Sweet Chestnut coppice. The remaining 20% is mixed native deciduous woodland presenting the highest conservation interest. In the coming years, Kent

Wildlife Trust will be working to remove the conifer plantations and restore the ancient woodland habitat and associated species.

Historically, much of the woods were harvested by coppicing, where young trees are cut to the ground and re-grow with multiple stems. The coppicing cycle was regular although the time between cuts varied depending on the use of the wood. In some instances, trees were coppiced at two or three years old for use as trellis and tool handles, fifteen-year-old trees were coppiced to make chestnut hop poles and sometimes over fifteen-year-old trees were harvested to produce fencing posts. Coppice also provided fuel, construction materials, furniture and charcoal - some of which was used by the Faversham gunpowder industry.

Coppicing creates temporary open spaces where the increase of sunlight and ground temperatures encourages plant growth and insect development which in turns benefits birds. Grassy glades, rides and pathways are other, more permanent ways, of providing woodland clearings which are so important to wildlife. Some glades can often be found where, in the past, woodmen stacked timber and converted the coppice material into poles, fencing, huardles, charcoal and other products. The rides were used by horses and carts to extract the wood products, and in some cases, wood rides were also created for pheasant shooting. Nowadays, clearings are created and maintained to provide habitat for a variety of invertebrates and a wide range of plants. The first few metres of the rides are mowed periodically so that they don't revert to scrub and the young trees on the edge of the ride are regularly coppiced to provide a progressive edge structure to the woods.

Heathland is an extremely scarce habitat in Kent, yet supports a wide range of wildlife not otherwise found. In some areas of the Blean where the soil is more acid, rides, glades and other clearings in the woodland form small patches of heath. Historically, heathland was much more widespread in the Blean and was mainly grazed by cattle. Nowadays, some areas of wooded heath are being restored and require the keeping of bramble, bracken and scrub in check by mowing, grazing, chemical control or a combination of these techniques.

The Radfall, (a drove road running between two woodbanks), which passes through Thornden Wood, is evidence of one of the routes taken by our Jutish forebears when cattle were moved through, on and off the Blean. Throughout the forest, the later mediaeval woodbanks and ditches indicate the importance which was once attached to the products of the Priory's woodlands, as part of their function was to exclude cattle and browsing livestock from the re-sprouting coppice.

Plants and animals of international importance:

West Blean and Thornden Wood are important for their avifauna. Summer visitors such as Nightjars are mainly found in recently coppiced areas and heathland patches where they build their nests on bare ground and hunt at dusk for moths and beetles and produce a strange churning trill often heard on warm still summer evenings. Nightingales like the dense thickets and scrub with thick foliage but are also found on the edges of clearings or rides, or clumps of bushes surrounded by heath or open space. Both of these species rely heavily on sympathetic woodland management. The continuity of suitable clear-fell and permanent open ground habitat is critical for the Nightjar and the thinning of woods to allow good light penetration to encourage and maintain a dense shrub layer and developing dense, species-rich coppice is vital to Nightingale populations in the Blean. Long-eared Owls are also known to breed and use the woodland. They favour thickets and copses and use nearby open country for hunting.

The Blean Wood complex is equally important for supporting a rich and nationally scarce invertebrate community. Insect species such as the scarce seven-spotted ladybird are only found near wood ants' nests in the south of England. The woods are also very important for butterfly species such as the White Admiral and the Heath Fritillary. The latter also known as the 'woodman's follower' is found in recent coppice as this favours Cow-Wheat which is the caterpillars' food plant. Over the past 50 years, coppicing has declined as local wood products become replaced with cheap imports and this very nearly caused this butterfly to become extinct. The Blean in itself hosts three quarters of the Heath Fritillary population of Great Britain. The management of rides and coppice rotations are the only way to protect this beautiful insect from vanishing for ever.

One of the most distinctive small mammals native to Britain and for which the management of the local woods is essential, is the Dormouse. With its thick furry tail, golden coloured fur and bulging black eyes, the dormouse is a nocturnal and tree-living species which mainly feeds on nectar, pollen, fruits, nuts and aphids, adapting its diet with the seasons. Dormice require a very specific habitat with a dense and unshaded shrub layer producing plenty of food but also some mature canopy trees. A wide variety of tree species is preferable, particularly ones producing berries or nuts. The Blean woods are a stronghold for the dormouse and the continuous coppice rotations are essential to the maintenance of the required habitat for them.

The bluebells and wood anemones which brighten the woods in the spring are of international importance. The British Bluebell represents 20% of the world's total population of the flower.

The Kent Wildlife Trust

The Good Life - Broad Oak Style

Edited transcript of the outcome of a taped conversation with Robert and Beryl Jackson by Linda Lodge, September 2006.

In 1953 Robert and Beryl Jackson bought the piece of land on Shalloak Road known as Priest's Meadow. This had mediaeval origins and included four acres of ancient woodland, as evidenced by the profusion of Dog's Mercury growing there. A dairy herd had been kept on the land in the 1940's by Sidney "Curly" Amos and his father and after the war a Mr Roberts had grown potatoes there.

After the war housing was very scarce and when they bought the land the Jacksons had to apply for planning permission to build a dwelling for agricultural workers' occupation. They purchased a Colt cedarwood bungalow from Biddenden and spent their evenings and weekends erecting it themselves, Harry Palmer from Sweechgate volunteering to teach them how to tile it and a young Mike Gisby worked on the shingle.

At the time Robert Jackson was still employed as Estate Manager farming mushrooms at Doddington near Faversham. An outbreak of a virus there prompted him to move away and farm for himself. Their two young children slept in the back of their Ford van whilst the Jacksons built the house in their spare time. The family moved in to the house in September 1955 even though it wasn't finished because their eldest daughter, Charlotte, had her fifth birthday in January and needed to be registered to start school in Sturry. Her parents still continued to work most of the night digging drains and so forth.

At first they grew cash crops, e.g. carrots, to generate income, but were unable to market them successfully. Because Robert was knowledgeable about mushrooms – indeed, he had written a text-book on the subject – MUSHROOM GROWING by Robert Louis Orr Jackson - they built two straw bale "houses" insulated with plastic and grew mushrooms, using the plentiful supply of farmyard manure. The spent mushroom compost went on the fruit.

Despite using a traction engine boiler to sterilise the mushroom houses the virus that had affected the Doddington farm finished this enterprise at Broad Oak. So, with a small loan from the bank, they planted four acres of soft fruit with varieties no commercial farmer would consider, including Royal Sovereign Strawberries and Himalayan Giant blackberries. The latter still grow on the land and now "Jackson's field" has the best blackberries in the parish.

As with the carrots and mushrooms, the problems were with picking and marketing. The fruit was taken sometimes to Sturry Station and by rail to Covent Garden – more often to Murrays in The Borough in London – but this proved very expensive. Not economic either at the end of the season – and years ahead of its time – was "Pick Your Own". It might not have paid then but it was well supported by the villagers. As ever innovative, Robert used the free peelings from chestnut coppicing to mulch raspberries. They acquired an old Ferguson tractor, although started on petrol, it was run on T.V.O. (tractor vapourising oil – a form of paraffin) on which Mike Gisby learnt to drive tractors.

Their next venture was into canning. They acquired a WI canning machine and taught themselves how to can fruit. The Metal Box Company were very helpful and sent Robert on a week's course in Birmingham to learn the arts of seaming, canning, sterilising, etc. They later hired them a canning machine, which the Jacksons eventually purchased. They began a mail order service under their own name label of "Harvest Days", advertising their twelve assorted tins in "The Times".

The Queen's grocer, Jackson's of Piccadilly, (no relation) analysed the canned fruit and pronounced it of excellent quality, hygiene and flavour and wanted to order five tons of each variety and use their own label. The bank advised them to employ people but would not fund this expansion. Mid-Kent Water refused permission for an artesian well (water there is only about three feet down) but allowed a one inch pipe (instead of half-inch) to bring water to the tanks for irrigating. During this venture into canning they were told that one of their tins had been seen on the shelves of the corner shop in "Coronation Street".

Wasps proved an ongoing problem and eventually the canning had to be done by night. By now Robert was supplementing his income by teaching science (he was a graduate of Wye College) at Barton Court, the Girls' Technical School in Canterbury. He began there part-time, then full time and eventually became Head of the Science Department. It still moves him to talk about how the women from the village came and helped pick the crop when he was struggling to teach by day and can at night – by now, with four young children.

After the farming Robert did printing at home – much of it for the flautist, Trevor Wye. He also ran a very successful printing club at Barton Court School with a shed for it built by parents in the grounds. With the aid of pupils in 1969 he produced a book called THIRTEEN CENTURIES OF BARTON COURT. He took early retirement at the age of sixty after a slight heart attack.

I think that the village had real pioneers in the Jacksons athough Robert maintains that his story is one of "make do and mend", and that lack of capital meant he couldn't do the things he wanted to do. His land has seen what he calls a "Marvellous regeneration" with hundreds of oak trees springing up where squirrels and birds had discarded them. Today there are tree preservation orders on most of them so they are safe.

Photograph by courtesy of The Kentish Gazette

Broad Oak Lions
Back Row: Edward Yeomans, William Harwood, Michael Hobbs, Jeff Eason, Maurice Collingwood, Frank Campbell, Colin Kennett, Sidney Ward.
Front row: Graham Harvey, Barry Ward, Douglas Garwood, Peter Campbell, Geoff Jones, George Harvey and Trevor Skewis.

Photograph by courtesy of The Kentish Gazette

Broad Oak Lions
Back row: Michael Hobbs, William Harwood, Jeff Eason, Maurice Collingwood, Douglas Garwood, Edward Yeomans, Trevor Skewis, Colin Kennett, Barry Ward, George Harvey, Geoff Jones
Front Row: Alec Hamilton, Tony Bubb, Malcolm Dunn, Billy Line, Ray Leach, Colin Gow, Tony Kennett, Graham Harvey, Kenny Harrison, Trevor Croxton, Martin Reynolds, Lee Elks, Roger Williams

Village Voices - 4

Edited interview with Norma Munday (née Whittaker) by Heather Stennett, October 2006

HS Tell me, Norma, how it was that you came to be living in my house in Broad Oak before we went to live there.

NM It's a bit of a long story but my father was a miner at Chislet Colliery and when the war broke we were living as a lot of miners did then in Ramsgate. Well, we were evacuated from there during Dunkirk week in 1940. They came at night to tell us that we – that is, the women and children - had to leave the next day. That was my Mother, Mary, me and Ellen - I can remember being carried over men lying on stretchers who had just come off the boats from France – and being taken to Dumpton Park station because all the other stations were used to get the troops away from the coast.

HS So where did you go to then?

NM Up to Newcastle in County Durham where my grandmother lived. But we didn't like it there and as soon as my Mother had had her baby – that would have been Janet – we all came back south.

HS What were your first memories of here

NM Walking up Sturry Hill. I thought I was never going to make it to the top. We'd had a horrendous journey from Newcastle on the train and I thought wherever Broad Oak was we were never going to get there. Then we got to the house and I loved every day that we lived there. Dad had got us two rooms in Broad Oak House from Mrs Alice Birch.

HS Where I live now.

NM That's right. My father, mother and my three sisters and me lived there. Mum and dad slept in the downstairs room – the one on the left as you go into the house. The windows had big shutters….

HS They still have.

NM We four girls slept in the upstairs room . We shared the kitchen with Mrs Birch – my Mum went out into the kitchen or scullery for cooking and washing – and it can't have been easy for anyone, could it?

HS No

NM I can't remember a bathroom, only an outside toilet, so we probably had a tin bath. The house wasn't on mains water then, you see.

HS Thank goodness it is now!

NM There was a big pump in the scullery which I thought was wonderful – I don't suppose that my mother did – and all the water for the day had to be pumped up. And there was a great big old sink and dresser. I remember it as being a lovely house because it was such an old one. We loved the back part of it – we used to run up the servant's stairs and, of course, played in the garden. That was our only playground because we were never allowed to play in the village. The gate at the end of the drive was our boundary. My Mother was very strict about that at first - I think because of the war – and anyway she thought Broad Oak rather rough and wild after the town - but all the other kids used to congregate at the stile so we soon got to know them anyway. Of course Mother worried what would happen if the sirens went off and we weren't there. We got on famously with the Birch girls – Betty, Hazel and Brenda - because of course we were all roughly the same age.

HS You'd have been there then when the unexploded bomb landed?

NM We were! We went over the road to the Roy family because my Dad and him were great friends. The girls had just got settled and put to bed on a big mattress on the floor – we didn't seem to have been there for more than five minutes – before we were got up again because they realised how big that bomb was and we were sent to Hoath School. Then all that area was evacuated and we were sent to a large house in Herne Bay while Broad Oak House was made safe.

HS What about school?

NM My younger sisters went to Sturry Primary School but I went to the Secondary School. First, we walked, rain or shine, then Bank's bus used to take us because of the air raids and things. Miss Cox was a favourite teacher and she used to run a Home Club – that's what I think she called it. Anyway she used to meet us on Saturdays and take us for walks. The first one was right down Mayton Lane and through the New Road to "The Fox and Hounds" on the road to Herne Bay. The next time it was from Mayton to where the University is now – I can still remember the lovely views.

HS What about Sundays?

NM On Sundays we'd put on our Sunday best and go for a walk. We'd go to the Chapel where Mr and Mrs Cooper were in charge. They were lovely people and the Sunday School was always full. Of course we were never allowed inside The Royal Oak but Dad would bring us back a Vimto on Saturday or Sunday evening. We used to buy eggs from Mrs Birch at "The Royal Oak" and vegetables from Mrs Pout and groceries from Ron Birch. And I remember scrumping in the orchards.

HS You weren't the only one

NM I had a flying visit to the haunted house – Broad Oak Lodge – when I was about fourteen. I got frightened after a few minutes and bolted out.

HS You weren't the only one to do that either

NM A great highlight was when Mrs Birch took me in her two-wheeled horse and trap to Westbere – it was the first time I'd been there and I still love it today. Then after a while we moved to a house of our own in Popes Lane. We had an air raid shelter in the garden there and then a Morrison – the one like a big steel table. Eventually we girls had a bed made up under the table so that we shouldn't be disturbed by the air raids. When I look back on those days my memories are all happy ones – I loved every minute of living in Broad Oak.

Field Map
by Les Moran

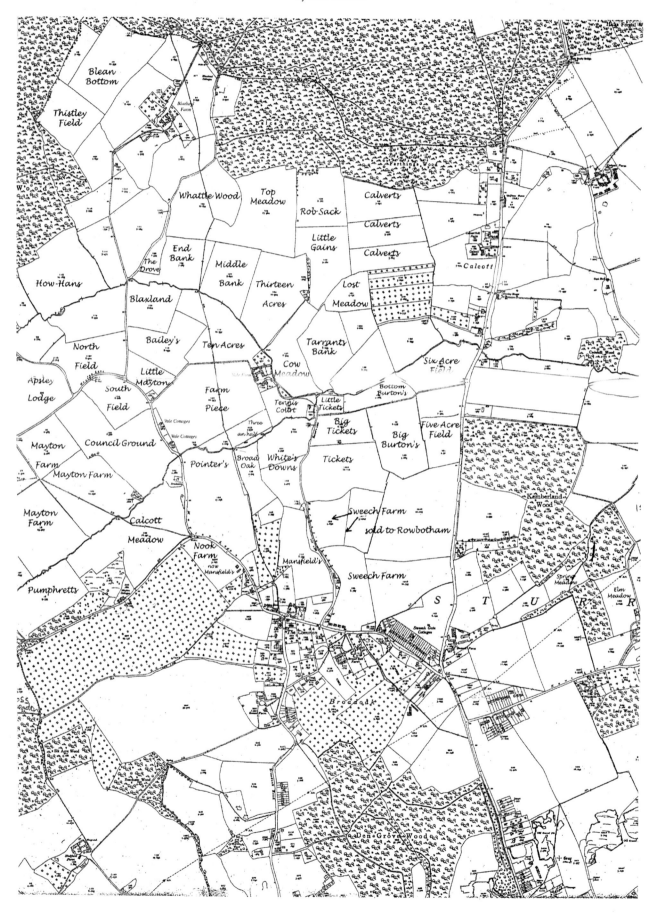